In search of the Holy Land

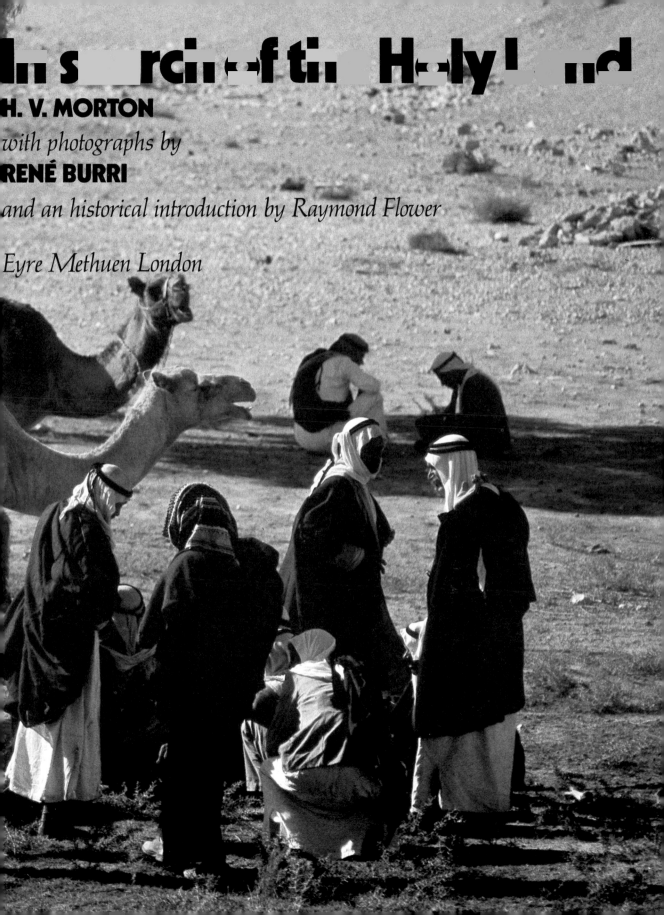

In Search of the Holy Land

H. V. MORTON

with photographs by
RENÉ BURRI

and an historical introduction by Raymond Flower

Eyre Methuen London

75989 50 .

First published 1979
by Eyre Methuen Limited
11 New Fetter Lane, London EC4P 4EE

Based on extracts taken from
In the Steps of the Master by H. V. Morton
(first published by Methuen 1937)
and selected by Christopher Derrick

This book was designed and produced in Great Britain
by LONDON EDITIONS LIMITED
30 Uxbridge Road, London W12 8ND

ISBN 0 413 45800 8

Printed and bound in Hong Kong by Mandarin Publishers Ltd

Contents

Publisher's Foreword

H. V. Morton's first travel books came out over half a century ago. As a young reporter he drove his bullnosed Morris to the farthest corners of Britain and Ireland, following no special plan but returning with material for his 'In Search' series. Later he travelled more widely, and perhaps his most famous books are the trilogy which emerged from his travels in the Middle East and which was published in the mid-1930s—*In the Steps of the Master*, *In the Steps of St Paul* and *Through Lands of the Bible*.

Their appeal to readers of any age is great and the reason for this simple. Travel writing at its best calls for imagination as much as for the writing skill to observe and report. Morton has imagination of two kinds: he can project himself back into history and capture distant events and the actors on stage at a particular place he visits; and when the people he meets are contemporaries, he understands them and their work with a sympathy they repay.

This volume presents extracts from H. V. Morton's *In the Steps of the Master* which complement the superb sequence of over 100 photographs in colour by René Burri.

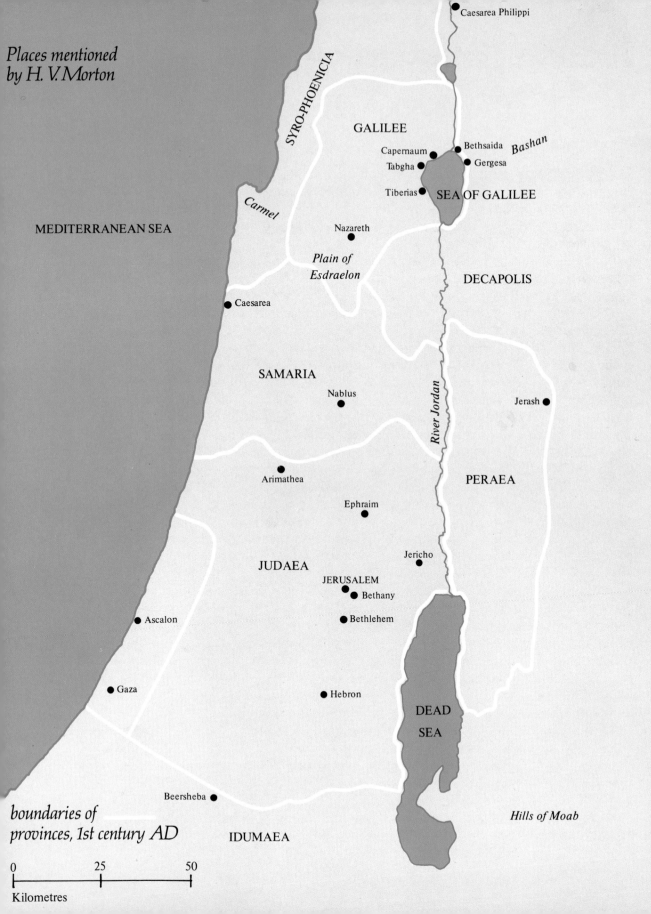

Places mentioned
by H. V. Morton

MEDITERRANEAN SEA

SYRO-PHOENICIA

Carmel

GALILEE

Caesarea Philippi

Bethsaida

Capernaum
Tabgha
Gergesa

Bashan

Tiberias

SEA OF GALILEE

Nazareth

Plain of
Esdraelon

DECAPOLIS

Caesarea

SAMARIA

Nablus

River Jordan

Jerash

Arimathea

PERAEA

Ephraim

Jericho

JUDAEA

JERUSALEM
Bethany

Ascalon

Bethlehem

Gaza

Hebron

DEAD
SEA

Beersheba

boundaries of
provinces, 1st century AD

IDUMAEA

Hills of Moab

0   25   50

Kilometres

Historical introduction

by Raymond Flower

IN 63 B.C. POMPEY captured Jerusalem and incorporated Palestine into the Roman Empire. But from much earlier times the stretch of land that ran "from Dan to Beersheba"—a distance of some 150 miles—had been inhabited by Semitic tribes who became known as the Yehudi, or men of Judah (although Judaea itself was only the area surrounding Jerusalem).

Living on the trade route between the great cultures of Egypt and Mesopotamia, these small tribes were inevitably dominated by their powerful neighbours. In the 15th century B.C. they were the vassals of Egypt, which, after expelling the Hyksos from the Nile Delta, had embarked on a series of conquests that took its empire as far as the Euphrates. During the high period of the New Kingdom, in fact, all Palestine was an Egyptian colony, administered by Egyptian officials.

Basically the Old Testament is a collection of writings which, after relating in mythical terms the story of Creation, tells the history of the Hebrew people from Abraham onwards. Thus *Exodus* recounts how the Israelites were freed from slavery in Egypt and escaped to Mount Sinai, where by covenant with the national god Jahweh they were given their laws and commandments. The book of *Joshua*—the first of the so-called historical books which record the story of the Israelites from the death of Moses to the Exile in Babylon—tells how they captured the promised land from the Philistines (as the indigenous Palestinians are still called in the Middle East) and divided it up among the twelve tribes. The books of *Samuel* describe the anointing of the first kings, Saul and David, by the prophet Samuel.

At the turn of the first millennium B.C. (so tradition has it), David completed the conquest by capturing Jerusalem, which became his stronghold and the central place of worship for the Israelite tribes. He was succeeded in about 970 B.C. by his son, Solomon, who built the great Temple of Jerusalem, from then onwards the high sanctum of Jewish faith. But for all the legendary wisdom and a business acumen that enabled him to control the trade between Asia and Africa, Solomon's extravagance ended in bankruptcy, while his policy of centralized government cut across the old tribal loyalties. On the accession of his son Rehoboam ("My father chastised you with whips, but I will chastise you with scorpions") rebellion broke out, and the country was split into the southern kingdom of Judah centered around Jerusalem, and the northern kingdom of Israel with its capital at Samaria.

This division was fatal, for once the Assyrians had conquered Syria in 721 B.C. they completely exterminated Israel (which became known as the Ten Lost Tribes.) And Judah hardly fared better. In 705 B.C. Sennacherib destroyed forty-six of its fortified towns and took most of the inhabitants off into captivity. Jerusalem itself only survived for another hundred years by paying a heavy bondage. No sooner, we are told, had the Babylonians captured the Assyrian capital of Nineveh than Nebuchadnezzar, faced with a revolt in Judah, unleashed his devastation on the holy city. By 587 David's kingdom lay in ruins.

Yet fifty years later the Persians, led by Cyrus, had defeated the Babylonians to become, in their turn, the masters of the ancient world. Unlike the Assyrians and the Babylonians before them, they believed in religious toleration. One of Cyrus' first acts was to allow the Jews to return to Jerusalem, and under Nehemiah the Temple was rebuilt around 515 B.C. Even so, many preferred to remain in the countries to which they had been exiled. This dispersion spread Judaism all over the then known world. "It was difficult", commented Josephus, "to find a single town in which there were no Jews."

But in 492 the Greek hoplites destroyed a third of the Persian army at Marathon, and the Persian fleet was overwhelmed at Salamis. As a result, Athens became the most powerful state in the Mediterranean until, weakened by the Peloponnesian war, Greece fell under the domination of the Macedonian king Philip. Sweeping through the Middle East, his son Alexander took Palestine in 332 B.C. Alexander's conquests had the effect of bringing Greek culture into the Middle East, and this Hellenic influence continued, at the expense of Judaism, even after the arrival of the Romans.

Such, briefly, is the historical background to the writings of the Old Testament.

If the thirty-nine books of the Old Testament formed part of the literature of the Hebrews, the twenty-seven books of the New Testament were written in demotic Greek and are concerned with the ministry of Jesus Christ and the spread of Christianity throughout the eastern Mediterranean.

Chronologically, the earliest mention of Jesus in Christian literature comes in the first Epistle to the Thessalonians, which scholars believe was written by St Paul less than twenty years after the crucifixion and some fifteen years before the gospel of St Mark. This, the shortest gospel, is thought to have been prompted by St Peter for the benefit of Christians in Rome who had to meet in secret. It tells how Jesus fulfilled the mission predicted by John the Baptist without actually declaring Himself to be the Messiah; how after captivating the people of Galilee with miracles and teachings He trained a small band of disciples to the point that they were convinced that He was the Christ, but at the same time incurred the suspicion and hatred of the Jewish religious establishment, who condemned Him as a blasphemer and handed Him over to the Romans as an illegal pretender to the Jewish throne. It was designed to reassure these little groups of clandestine believers, themselves persecuted by the Emperor Nero, that Jesus was indeed the Saviour.

Side by side with Mark's gospel there existed another account of Jesus' life and sayings, possibly noted down by the apostle Matthew, which has now disappeared and is referred to by scholars as "Q" (from the German *Quelle*, or source.) Both the gospel of St Matthew (which may have been connected with Matthew, but was almost certainly not written by him) and that of St Luke (traditionally the physician who accompanied Paul on his missionary journeys) used this source along with Mark's narrative to give a fuller account of Jesus' ministry on earth.

St John's gospel, on the other hand, is thought to have been written by John—"the disciple whom Jesus loved"—when a very old man, perhaps at the request of the early leaders of the Church, to explain the true meaning of Jesus' sayings and actions and to substantiate His divine claim. Unlike the other evangelists, John speaks of a ministry not just in Galilee and northern Palestine, but also in Judaea when Jesus visited Jerusalem for religious feasts, stressing His rejection by the Jews in the holy city. These four different word portraits give the earliest and most reliable account of Christ's life and teaching.

At the time that Jesus was born, Herod the Great had been reigning for over thirty years. Arab by birth, Jew by religion, Hellenic by sympathy and Roman by allegiance, this authoritarian monarch had brought peace to Palestine after a century of disquiet following the Maccabean revolt. Rome now ruled the whole of the Mediterranean, and Herod's policy had been to play along with the Romans. He knew that there was no possibility of gaining complete independence for Judaea, and he regarded collaboration with the super-power as the price of survival and prosperity. But although he protected the Jewish faith and rebuilt the Temple, it was obvious from his Graeco-Roman enthusiasms that he did not feel wholeheartedly a Jew. For this his subjects never forgave him, and their hostile propaganda—such as the story of the massacre of the infants in Bethlehem, which he was quite capable of ordering but almost certainly didn't—has distorted his memory until this day.

Herod's kingdom was divided into three parts among his surviving sons, as directed in his final death-bed will and approved by the Emperor Augustus. Thus Archelaus became Ethnarch of Judaea; Antipas was given Galilee; while Philip got the mountain territories that are now on the Syrian border. After ten years Archelaus was banished to France and his principality became a minor Roman province, which as time wore on was progressively more disturbed by Jewish underground resistance. During and after the governorship of Pontius Pilate (A.D. 26–36) there were almost continuous acts of violence and bloodshed. This was the political background during Jesus' lifetime.

Of His early life we know little, beyond that He was born in Bethlehem, was probably taken to Egypt as a baby, and grew up in Nazareth, perhaps helping His father as a carpenter. For the Passover, He would have gone to Jerusalem each year with His family, and Luke gives a pleasant glimpse of the boy Jesus at the Temple in serious discussion with the rabbis, who were amazed by His knowledge. But it was not until He was over thirty that He left His village and went to Judaea to be baptised by John. Then after forty days in the wilderness—the barren steep hills on each side of the Dead Sea where He was tempted by the devil—He returned to Galilee and began His teaching. Spurned by the strict Jews of Nazareth who found it hard to believe that the young man they had known for so long had any special message to give them ("A prophet is not without honour, save in his own country, and in his own house"), Jesus moved to Capernaum and made that His centre. From here, Matthew tells us, He "went about all Galilee, teaching in their synagogues, and preaching the gospel of the kingdom, and healing all manner of sickness and all manner of disease among the people." Around Him He gathered a group of disciples, and as His fame spread crowds flocked to hear what He had to say. They followed

Him into the desert, and on the shores of Lake Galilee they were so numerous that He was forced to get into a boat and speak to them across the water.

From the synoptic gospels it would appear that the greater part of His ministry took place in Galilee, though John mentions journeys to Jerusalem. Matthew records that Jesus gave His twelve disciples "authority over unclean spirits, to cast them out, and heal every disease and infirmity among the people" and sent them out through the countryside to teach and to heal. Inevitably these activities, and above all the miracles that were attributed to Jesus, aroused the envy and hostility of the established Jewish authorities whose rigid adherence to the Law of Moses He criticized on humanitarian grounds. Worse still, Herod Antipas, the Tetrarch of Galilee and Peraea, who had already beheaded John the Baptist, began to suspect that He was a trouble-maker and maybe even a "guerilla" leader. So Jesus left Galilee and spent some time around Tyre and Sidon, which were outside Antipas' jurisdiction.

If the gospels do not make it clear what route He followed, they record how on the road to Caesarea Philippi Jesus asked His disciples point blank who they thought He really was. To which Peter replied: "Thou art the Christ, the Son of the living God." The gospels relate that a few days later the "Transfiguration" took place up a high mountain—which may have been Mount Hermon, near Caesarea Philippi, though some authorities suggest that it was on Mount Tabor, near Nazareth. Soon after this, Jesus began His ultimate journey to Jerusalem, travelling slowly through Judaea. According to John, He spent some time at Bethany, only a short distance from the capital, and also preached on the east bank of the Jordan. At Bethany He brought His friend Lazarus back to life—an action that so enraged the Chief Priests that they made up their minds to kill Him. Finally, after moving for a short while to Ephraim, He returned to Jerusalem and His Fate.

While these places are indelibly connected with Jesus, the rest of the land must have been well known to Him too. In the course of His lifetime He must have gazed on most of the scenery that we can still see, and have walked along ancient tracks that are still in use. But not only does the configuration of the landscape remain as it was in Jesus' day or indeed in the earliest times of the Old Testament, the actual way of life, outside the urban centres, has so little changed that it is possible even now to recapture the biblical scenes. This sense of continuity is one of the great charms of the Mediterranean countries. In the Holy Land the Bible still lives on in the daily round of the rural inhabitants.

Abraham, we are told, had asses and camels. Donkeys remain a favourite form of village transport and camels still plod through the towns with a haughty disregard for the internal combustion engine. In the hills around Jerusalem, shepherds continue to watch their flocks, and teams of oxen plough between the olive trees drawing the same type of plough that was used by the Israelites. The grapes that Moses' scouts found on Mount Hebron are the forebears of those that now produce the Richon Le Zion wine; the pomegranates and figs are just as abundant today. The fig, mentioned in *Genesis* 3:7 was often planted to support the vines and produce a shady arbour: farmers still sit, as Micah described, "every man under his vine and under his fig tree"

(4:4). The palms, whose leaves were used as a symbol of victory and rejoicing (and, more practically, to make baskets) still grow in profusion around Jericho. The olive, no less a symbol of good news to us than it was to Noah (*Genesis* 8:11), is still the most characteristic tree of the Holy Land, where its gnarled trunk and silver-grey foliage flourish on the rocky hillsides. And the fishermen still cast their nets from rowing boats on the Sea of Galilee, as Andrew and Peter were doing when Jesus called them.

Nor, despite the encroachment of urban industrialization, have the villages themselves changed much over the centuries. Many are still a haphazard jumble of square box-like houses, built in yellowish stone or roughly plastered brick with a small courtyard for the goats and sheep, a store and a living-room furnished with little more than a rush mat on which the family squats to eat and lies down to sleep. In the little shops that open out on to narrow, twisting alleys, the metal workers, potters, weavers, carpenters, bakers, blacksmiths and tanners still carry on their trades. If the great buildings of antiquity that Jesus knew are now in ruins or replaced by later structures, the bustle and smells of the biblical village are with us today.

In the centuries that have passed since Jesus lived, the process of man's evolution has altered much of the globe. Yet to an astonishing degree the fundamentals of life remain constant. Indeed to read the scriptures is to share a cultural experience with all the generations that have gone by. Of the billions of words that have been published since printing began, it is unlikely that any single person can read more than a tiny fraction. But it is almost certain that he will have read a large part of the Bible.

No other book in the history of the world has ever had such an impact on man's imagination. Both Christians and Jews recognize the Old Testament as a record of the long process by which God revealed Himself and His design, and many of its stories are reflected in the Koran. The great point of encounter is the belief in One God.

To be sure, the word of the Old Testament is no longer taken as literally as it was in the middle ages. Yet if historians have since taken a more sophisticated view about the accuracy of the Bible, realizing that the Old Testament was drawn from documents written over a period of centuries in a world used to picture language, the most recent scholarship is tending towards the belief that, allegories apart, most of the historical statements are indeed correct. It is the interpretation of the old Hebrew scriptures—many of which are corroborated by the beautiful religious picture scripts of the New Kingdom in Egypt—that have often been at fault.

For Christians, Jesus Christ is the central figure of the whole Bible, and although the gospels can be read in a single evening, the message they contain—humanity, as opposed to ritual worship, and God's love for mankind—has inspired much of the world for two thousand years. Too often, though, Christ's simple, authoritative teachings have been blurred by dogma; and although the scriptures have inspired great art, the stained glass of a cathedral and the bewitching paintings of the Renaissance can easily put one's eye out of focus. Anyone who has lived in the Middle East knows how the biblical scenes that can be seen and experienced all around one lead to an understanding of the Bible, and bring it to life. In such surroundings, its teachings assume a vivid new clarity.

Nearly half a century ago, H. V. Morton visited the Holy Land to travel, as he put it, "In the Steps of the Master"—the title he gave to his best-loved book. And when in 1963 the late Paul VI became the first Pope to have seen the traditional birthplace of Christ for himself, René Burri began dedicating himself to the task of illustrating, with his camera, the eternal background against which the scriptures were enacted. By bringing together Burri's pictures and Morton's impressions it is hoped to contribute, however modestly, to a greater appreciation of the Holy Land and of the Bible.

Mosaic pavement,
Caesarea

Nativity and Boyhood

Bethlehem and Nazareth

THE ROAD WAS like any other road in the Holy Land. The sky was a hot lid above it. The snapping of grasshoppers in the olive groves was a steady rhythm in the heat.

The road was white with the dust of powdered limestone, a floury dust which the heels of the donkeys kicked up in clouds; but the soft feet of the camels hardly moved it, as they passed silent as shadows. White stone walls lay on either side, and behind them the stony terraces, planted with olive trees, lifted themselves in sharp white ridges against the darkness of the sky. Little brown lizards with the watchful heads of frogs lived in the chinks of the stones. They would come out to lie in the sun, still as the stones, except for a quick beating in their throats. Sometimes I could go to within a yard of them, and would be just about to touch them with an olive twig, when, swift as a whiplash flicked out of the dust, they would be gone.

The heat was a nervous tension enclosing the world. All sounds were an invasion, except that of the grasshoppers, which was the palpitating voice of the heat. A shepherd boy piped somewhere on the hill, playing a maddening little tune without beginning or end, a little stumbling progress up and down a scale, like the ghost of a waterfall. And the white road led on under the sun.

It was, as I have said, just like any other road in the Holy Land. But there was one thing that marked it out from all other roads in the world. It was the road to Bethlehem.

As I walked on, I thought that travel there is different from travel in any other part of the world because it exists already in our imagination before we start out. From our earliest years it begins to form in our minds side by side with fairyland, so that it is often difficult to tell where one begins and the other ends. Therefore the Holy Land of reality is always in conflict with the imaginary Holy Land, so violently at times that many people cannot relinquish this creature of the imagination without a feeling of bereavement. That is why some people go away disillusioned from the Holy Land. They are unable, or unwilling, to reconcile the real with the ideal.

Any truthful account of travel in the Holy Land must mention this conflict. Every day you hear travellers say, as they visit some place: "I never imagined it quite like that," or "I always thought of it in a different way."

And as I went on to Bethlehem I remembered a place hushed in snow where shepherds wrapped in thick cloaks watched their flocks under the frosty stars. There was a little shelter in this place in which beasts stamped in their stalls and blew the fog of their breath into the cold air. On the straw near the mangers, sitting in exquisite detachment, was a Mother with a gold circle about her head and a little Child. The stars shone coldly, and through the air came a sound of far-off bells.

I know perfectly well that this picture was edged with gilt. It was my own private little vision of Bethlehem, something that has been with me all my life, something made up in my mind from Christmas cards sent to me when I was a child, from pictures that I loved before I could read, something formed by the piety and reverence which a cold northern land has cast round the story of the Nativity. Every Christian nation has translated the story of Christ into its own idiom and cradled Him in its own barns. The great mediaeval painters have, each man in his own way, painted in the national background of his own country and his own time. And we who come from Europe come from an enchanted country to the bare rocks and crags of reality.

I walked along in the airless heat, sorry to say farewell to this little picture of mine; and the heat of the white road to Bethlehem quivered like fire over the limestone walls and beat like the breath of a furnace upon the grey little olive trees and shone through the greenness of the uncurling fig leaves.

The white houses cluster on the hill like a group of startled nuns. They stand on the edge of the road and gaze down into a pit of heat. Where the striped terraces end and the bare rock begins, the last olive trees seem to be struggling desperately to run back up the stony terraces away from the heat and the sterility of the rock. The white houses watch them with open mouths that are doors, and startled eyes that are windows. And the hot sunlight beats down from the blue sky.

Above the flat, white roofs rise the bell-towers of convents and orphanages and monasteries. There is always a bell ringing in the heat. If it is not the bell of the Salesian Fathers, it may be the bell of the Sisters of St. Vincent de Paul. At the bottom of the road that leads up to this white hill-town is a notice-board which absurdly pins this region to reality: "Bethlehem Municipal Boundary," it says. "Drive slowly."

The traveller, approaching Bethlehem with his mind on St. Luke and Botticelli, pauses in surprise before this board because it has never before occurred to him that Bethlehem could be confined by municipal boundaries. It seems to him, at first, almost sacrilege that Bethlehem should possess a mayor and a municipality. Then, when he ceases to feel and begins to think, it occurs to him that the Mayor of Bethlehem is a wonderful symbol. He is a sign of an almost terrifying continuity of human life. His predecessors in office extend back before the time of Christ into the days of the Old Testament, and probably into dim, distant regions of legend. Bethlehem is typical of the strange immutability of these towns of the Holy Land. Wave after wave of conquest has swept over them without, apparently, making much difference to them. Bethlehem has known the Jews, the Romans, the Arabs, the Crusaders, the Saracens and the Turks. They have all erected their notice-boards on her boundaries. And now there is one in English at the bottom of the hill asking you to "drive slowly."

I once read a story, I think it was written by H. G. Wells, in which someone discovered a door in a very ordinary wall which led into the Garden of the Hesperides. The memory of it came to me in Bethlehem when I encountered a door in a massive wall. It was so low that even a dwarf would have to bend his head in order to pass through it. On the other side of it was the Church of the Nativity. They say in Bethlehem that all the doors into this church were walled up long ago, except this one, which was made low in order to prevent the infidel from riding into the building on horseback and slaying the worshippers.

But no sooner had I bent my head and stepped across than I straightened up—in Rome! It was the Rome of Constantine the Great, or, perhaps I should say, New Rome. It was the biggest surprise I had had in the Holy Land. I expected the usual ornate church, the dark, burdened altars, the confused stairs and passages of a reconstructed building, and here I was in a cold, austere Roman basilica. Massive Corinthian pillars made of some dull red stone upheld the roof and divided the church into a nave and aisles. I was in the church that Constantine the Great built long ago as a sign that he had become a Christian. Surely one of the marvels of the Holy Land is the fact that this church should have survived the dangers that have swept the other buildings of its time to dust? Here it is, the earliest Christian church in use to-day, and more or less as it left the hands of its builders. On the walls are the remains of dim gold mosaics.

left: Jericho

below: Bethlehem

overleaf: Church of the Nativity, Bethlehem

Church of the Nativity

opposite: Beersheba market

page 28: Bethlehem, where "the white houses cluster on the hill like a group of startled nuns"

The church is built above a cave which was recognized as the birthplace of Jesus Christ two centuries before Rome became a Christian state. The grotto must have been sacred to Christians in the time of Hadrian. In order to defame it, as he tried to defame Golgotha, he built over it a temple to Adonis. Constantine pulled down this temple and built this present church in its place. There seems to me something so touchingly formal about it, as if the Roman Empire did not yet quite understand this new faith, but was making a first, puzzled genuflection in its direction. One feels that these pillars are really the pillars of a temple to Jupiter.

A service was in progress. I thought the choir was filled with nuns, but they were ordinary Bethlehem women wearing the tall veiled headdress of the town. Beneath the high altar is the cave which tradition claims as the spot where Christ was born. It is entered by flights of steps set on each side of the choir. On the way down I had to press myself against the dark little staircase as two Greek monks, black of eye and beard, came up in a cloud of incense.

Fifty-three silver lamps hardly lighten the gloom of the underground cavern. It is a small cave about fourteen yards long and four yards wide. Its walls are covered with tapestry that reeks of stale incense. If you draw this tapestry aside, you see that the walls are the rough, smoke-blackened walls of a cave. Gold, silver and tinsel ornaments gleam in the pale glow of the fifty-three lamps.

I thought I was alone in the cavern until someone moved in the darkness, and I noticed the policeman who is always on duty to prevent disputes between the Greek and the Armenian priests. This church, like the Church of the Holy Sepulchre, suffers from divided ownership. It is in the hands of the Latins, the Greeks, and the Armenians.

So jealous are the various churches of their rights that even the sweeping of the dust is sometimes a dangerous task, and there is a column in which are three nails, one on which the Latins may hang a picture, one on which the Greeks may do so, and a neutral nail on which no sect may hang anything.

In the floor there is a star, and round it a Latin inscription which says: "Here Jesus Christ was born of the Virgin Mary." The removal of this star years ago led to a quarrel between France and Russia which blazed into the Crimean War.

Such truths may seem terrible; but this, alas, is an imperfect world. It is therefore necessary, as you stand in the Church of the Nativity, or in the Holy Sepulchre, to try and forget the frailties of men and to look beyond them to the truth and the beauty which they seem to obscure.

As I stood in this dark, pungent cavern I forgot, I am afraid, all the clever and learned things written about the Nativity by German professors, and I seemed to hear English voices singing under a frosty sky:—

> O come, all ye faithful,
> Joyful and triumphant,
> O come ye, O come ye to Bethlehem.

How different is this dark little cave under a church from the manger and the stable of one's imagination! As a child, I thought of it as a thatched English barn with wooden troughs for oats and hay, and a great pile of fodder on which the Wise Men knelt to adore "the new-born Child." Down the long avenues of memory I seemed to hear the waits singing in the white hush of Christmas night:—

While shepherds watched their flocks by night,
All seated on the ground,
The Angel of the Lord came down,
And glory shone around.

There was a rhythmic chinking sound on the dark stairs. A Greek priest, with a black beard curled like that of an Assyrian king, came slowly into the cavern swinging a censer. The incense rolled out in clouds and hung about in the candle flames. He censed the altar and the Star. Then, in the most matter-of-fact way, he genuflected and went up into the light of the church.

Beneath the church is a warren of underground passages. In one of them, a dark rock chamber, St. Jerome conducted a number of his keen controversies and translated the Vulgate.

But I found my way back to the cavern where the incense drifts in the lamp flames. The grotto was full of little children, silently standing two by two on the stairs. They came forward, knelt down and quickly kissed the stone near the star. Their little faces were very grave in the candle-light. Some of them closed their eyes tightly and whispered a prayer.

No sooner had the last of them gone, than I heard the chink-chink of the censer; and into the gloom of the Grotto of the Nativity came again a Greek priest like an Assyrian king.

There are a number of old houses in Bethlehem built over caves in the limestone rock. These caves are exactly the same as the sacred grotto under the high altar of the Church of the Nativity, and they are probably as ancient. No one who has seen these houses can doubt that Jesus was born in one of them, and not in the stable of European tradition.

I suppose the idea that Christ was born in a stable was suggested by St. Luke's use of the word "manger." To the Western mind this word presupposes a stable or a barn, or some outbuilding separate from the house and used as a shelter for animals. But there is nothing in St. Luke to justify this.

These primitive houses in Bethlehem gave me an entirely new idea of the scene of the Nativity. They are one-room houses built over caves. Whether these caves are natural or artificial I do not know: they are level with the road, but the room above them is reached by a flight of stone steps, perhaps fifteen or twenty. The caves are used to this day as stables for the animals, which enter from the road level. There are, in most of them, a stone trough, or manger, cut from the rock, and iron rings to which the animals

are tied during the night.

The family occupy the upper chamber, separated only by the thickness of the rock floor from the cave in which the animals sleep.

Now, if Joseph and Mary had visited the "inn" at Bethlehem and found it full, there would have been no stable for them to go to, because the "inns," or khans, in the time of Christ were merely open spaces surrounded by a high wall and a colonnade under whose arches were rooms for the travellers. The animals were not stabled in the European sense, but were gathered together in the centre of the enclosure. The Greek word *katalyma* used by St. Luke, and translated as "inn," would be more exactly rendered as "guest-chamber."

Therefore I believe we must imagine the Nativity to have taken place in one of these old cave-houses of Bethlehem. The guest-chamber, or upper room, which it was the Jewish custom to offer to travelling Jews, was evidently already occupied, and therefore the host did his best by offering to the Holy Family shelter of the downstairs room, or cave.

As the road sweeps across the broad green Plain of Jezreel and climbs into the mountains on which Nazareth is enthroned, the visitor can think of nothing but the boyhood of Jesus. Every rock and every hill is important, for these things do not change and He must have known these rocks and these hills. Looking back, the great plain stretching to the sky and the outward thrust spur of Carmel to the west are intensely significant.

When the road straightens out at the top of the hill and runs towards the snow-white houses of Nazareth, towards the thousands of spear-like cypresses, the terraces of fig and olive trees, the town is exactly as one likes to imagine it. Even Bethlehem is not more satisfying to the eye.

One is shown all kinds of holy places in Nazareth, but perhaps the only one that really convinces is the Virgin's Fountain. This is, and ever has been, the only water supply of Nazareth. The stream gushes out of the mountain and runs through a conduit to a public fountain where women fill petrol tins with water all day long. The Greeks have built a church above the source of this spring and, when you go down into the darkness of this sanctuary, you can hear the water bubbling up from the rock. This must be the spring from which the Virgin Mary drew water.

Down in the narrow streets of the town I found a

whole street of carpenters busily at work sawing wood, and using planes and chisels. These men, who work in archways open to the street, are mostly Christian Arabs, and a characteristic product of the trade is a wooden cradle on rockers which is common all over Galilee. These cradles are always painted blue, a colour which is believed to ward off evil spirits.

As one stands among the wood shavings of these little shops in Nazareth, the old question: "Did Jesus work at the carpenter's bench?" comes to one's mind. St. Mark calls Him "the carpenter," but St. Matthew, "the carpenter's son." An attempt has often been made, by an examination of the similes used by Jesus, to prove that He was a practical carpenter during the years of His life of which we know nothing. But these references are too slender for anyone, except a Biblical critic, to found an opinion.

There are His sayings "Cleave the wood and there you will find me"; "If they do these things in a green tree, what shall be done in the dry"; and there is the similitude of the mote and the beam. Surely to these we might add the parable of the house built upon sand?

I was interested to discover that the carpenters of modern Nazareth are of two kinds: the modern carpenter, who makes furniture and prepares wood for the builder, and the old-fashioned carpenter.

If Jesus did adopt the trade of Joseph, we must imagine Him working as the old-fashioned carpenters of Nazareth work to-day. The methods have not changed.

Their clients are the small farmers and the agricultural labourers of the district. They contract to make, and to keep in repair for a year, all the agricultural tools of a village. Payment is made in grain, so much for each yoke of oxen. At the end of

Nazareth – "Even Bethlehem is not more satisfying to the eye"

overleaf: road near Jerusalem

the year the village carpenter goes round at threshing time to all his clients and draws his pay in barley, wheat, sesame or olives.

In the old days these carpenters had more work to do. They used to make doors and window-frames from the dwarf oaks of Bashan, a wood called by the Arabs, *Siindian*. But this branch of their work has been monopolised by the modern craftsmen, who can do much cheaper carpentry in Austrian wood.

I came to one dark little hovel in which a very old man, squatting on the floor among a pile of aromatic wood chips and shavings, was using a primitive hand drill. Round about him were various yokes and ploughs and agricultural tools. He was the real old-fashioned carpenter of the Holy Land, a character who has existed unchanged since the invasion of the Israelites.

While I was exploring the street of the carpenters, I recalled a rather significant remark of Justin Martyr, who wrote that Jesus, "when amongst men, worked as a carpenter, making ploughs and yokes, thus teaching the marks of righteousness and making an active life."

There is an ancient and curious legend to the effect that the Emperor Julian, the apostate who tried to crush Christianity and bring back the pagan gods, once asked a Christian: "What is the Carpenter doing now?" And the Christian answered, "He is making a coffin." The point of the anecdote is that Julian died soon afterwards.

There seem, among the early Christians, to have been some men who believed that Jesus practised the craft, and others who, piously considering that such humble work lowered His dignity, attempted to disguise the fact. But there can be little doubt that Joseph the Carpenter was exactly like the village carpenters in Galilee to-day, whose skill ministers to a whole village and whose reward comes at harvest time.

left: Bethlehem

above: near Hebron

Baptism, Temptation and Ministry

Jordan, Jericho and Galilee

I TOOK A ROAD straight across the hills and hummocks towards the place of Christ's baptism. It was not really a road: it was an ill-defined cart-track that lost itself in thorn bushes, found itself in holes and swamps and went on twisting and winding towards the thin belt of green that marks the course of the Jordan.

No one knows where the place of the Baptism was, neither do we know where "Bethany beyond Jordan" was. But the place I discovered among the tamarisk and the willows is that which has been hallowed by centuries of pious pilgrimage. In the old days before the War, when Russia was "Holy Russia," thousands of pilgrims used to come down to this place to plunge into the Jordan, wearing white gowns which they took home to keep as their shrouds. To-day there are few pilgrims. The custom of bathing at this spot, or somewhere near it, goes back to the most remote times. It was known to the Pilgrim of Bordeaux, who visited the Holy Land in the Roman era—about the year 333 A.D., and one evening in the year 1172 Theodoric saw sixty thousand persons plunge into the river at this spot.

The Jordan surprised me. I felt that I was standing on the bank of some English stream, perhaps the Avon in Warwickshire high up beyond the mill in flood-time. I cannot say why I should have felt this, because the banks of the Jordan are thick with exotic, foreign trees and shrubs such as tamarisk and a thin reed, like bamboo. I think it was the way a group of willows dropped their leaves in the water exactly as they do when the Avon floods the meadows round Stratford-on-Avon in March. And as I looked at the Jordan touching the willow leaves and moving them the way of the current, I seemed to be back again in the great happiness of my youth, sitting upon an old green wall near Holy Trinity. There is something slow and gentle and small about the Jordan as it swings round the bend beside the place of the Baptism, something, as I say, very home-like that made me think of those devout paintings on the walls of Venice and Florence in which men have painted Bethlehem and Nazareth like their own towns. It seemed to me that there should be a lesson in this, but a better moralist than myself would have to make it: that a man should travel across the world to see the holy Jordan, and discover it to be just like the little stream at home that runs at the bottom of his garden.

I thought how true this vision of mine was, and how it would probably be contradicted by every tourist who has seen the milky-blue and sandy whirlpools of this river. For the Jordan does flow in every part of the Christian world. Some little drop finds its way into every font at every baptism.

It is an extraordinary commentary on the smallness of the Holy Land that Jesus in the course of His missionary journeys was never more than a hundred and thirty miles distant from Jerusalem. This was on the occasion of His departure to the borders of Tyre and Sidon. The smallness of the country is such that from many of the high ridges of Judaea all the boundaries are clearly visible: snow-capped Hermon to the north, the sandy desert to the south, the Mediterranean Sea to the west, and the high ridge of the Trans-Jordan mountains to the east.

When the Bible says that Moses was shown all the Promised Land from the top of Mount Nebo, it is literally true. From this height, four thousand feet above the Dead Sea, he could see the outline of the entire country. And there are many other mountains from which the same tremendous panorama is visible.

The Life which has meant more to humanity than any other life was, therefore, lived within an astonishingly small compass, and the faith that has created the modern world was born in a country about the size of Wales, and cradled in a part of it— Galilee—that is far smaller than Devonshire.

Jesus, in the words of *Acts*, "went about doing good." But when we examine the details of these journeys in the Gospels we realise, perhaps with surprise, that the towns and villages which He visited number only eighteen. It is obvious that during the thirty odd years of His earthly life, Christ must have known this small Holy Land from end to end. The Gospels, apart from the flight into Egypt mentioned only by St. Matthew, and the disputation with the elders mentioned only by St. Luke, deal with a brief period in the life of Christ which scholars have estimated to be from eighteen months to three and a half years. These are the years of the Baptism, the Galilean Ministry, and the Crucifixion. How Jesus spent the greater part of His life is a mystery. Not one word has been recorded about it. Some scholars regard this as the most provoking problem in history, while others believe it to be an intentional mystery.

In the time of Jesus the Sea of Galilee was one of the busiest centres of life in the country, and the western shore was ringed with towns and villages. The ruler of the province had his palace on the hill above Tiberias. The lake was crowded with ships.

One has always imagined that Jesus preached His Gospel to simple country-folk in a remote part of the Holy Land where no whisper of the outside world ever interrupted the immortal current of His thought. In actual fact His Ministry was conducted not only in the most cosmopolitan region in the country, but also in a territory where the ancient trade routes from Tyre and Sidon on the west, and the old caravan roads from Damascus on the north-east, as well as the great imperial highways, met together and branched out over the country. Galilee was on the main road of the ancient world, a half-way house between Damascus and the Egyptian frontier, on one hand, and between Antioch and Jerusalem on the other.

When Jesus walked the roads of Galilee He met the long caravans working southward across the fords of Jordan; He saw the sun gleam on the spears of Roman maniples and cohorts; He met bands of Phoenician merchants travelling into Galilee; encountered the litters and chariots of the great, and saw the bands of strolling players and jugglers and gladiators bound for the gay Greek cities of the Decapolis.

The shadow of this world falls across the pages of the New Testament. Jesus, walking the roads of Galilee, is walking the modern world, with its money-changers and its tax-collectors, its market-places and its unhappy rich men. When we think of Him beside the Sea of Galilee, we must not imagine Him as retired from the world, preaching His Gospel to a few faithful, simple souls: we must realise that He had chosen to live among people of many nations and upon one of the main highways of the Roman Empire.

Galilee is one of the sweetest words I know. Even were it possible to dissociate it from the Ministry of Jesus, it would still be a lovely word whose three syllables suggest the sound of lake water lapping a shore. It is as soft as the word Judaea is hard, as gentle as Judaea is cruel. It is not necessary to visit the Holy Land to appreciate the rocky harshness of "Judaea" or to hear the water falling from the oars in "Galilee."

The meaning of the word Galilee is "Ring, or Region, of the Gentiles." The Hebrew word *Galil* means a circlet, or anything that is round. The district was never entirely Jewish, even in the earliest times. Ten cities of Galilee were given by Solomon to Hiram, King of Tyre, as part payment for the building of the Temple, and the invasion of the Gentile population continued in later times. When Jesus went to live beside Galilee, the western shore of the lake was dotted with a ring of towns and fishing villages in which the non-Jewish element was very strong. The pure-blooded Orthodox Jew of Jerusalem looked down with contempt upon the Galilean and made fun of his dialect and of the way he pronounced the gutturals. Those who stood in the court of the High Priest's house after the arrest of Jesus detected that St. Peter was a follower of Christ. "Thou art a Galilean," they said, "for thy speech bewrayeth thee." Amusing errors in grammar and absurd mistakes due to mispronunciation were constantly cited by the superior Judaeans as proof of the stupid, yokel character of the Galileans.

It seems, however, that in freeing itself from the Rabbinic rigidity of Judaea, Galilee found room for idealism and an intense nationalism. While the Judaean had bound himself up in formalism, the Galilean had become speculative and independent. It was not chance that led Jesus to sow the seeds of His teaching on the receptive shores of Galilee. . . .

I got back to Jericho as the afternoon sun was sinking. I was anxious to be on the mountain road before dark, but I was also determined to climb the

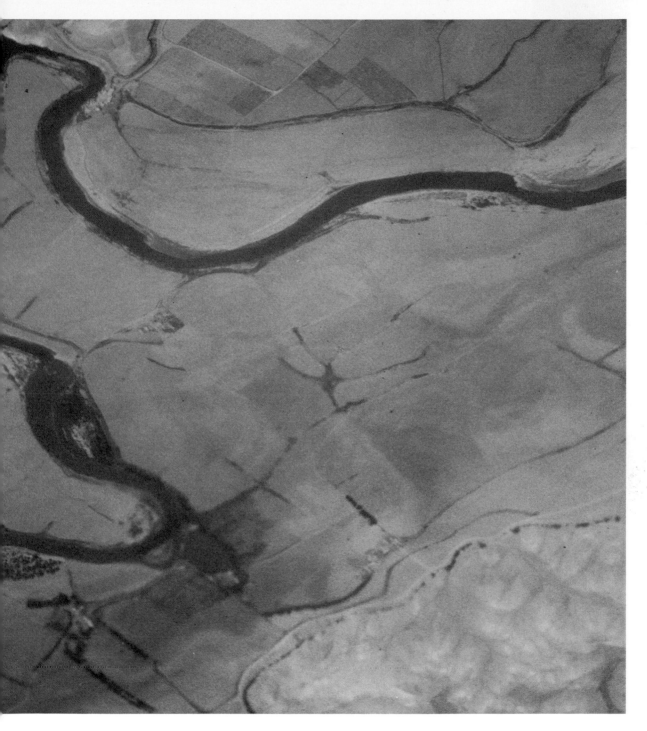

"In the centre meanders a serpentine streak of green. It is formed by the tamarisks, the willows and the green bushes that follow the Jordan's two-hundred-mile windings"

overleaf: the Jordan near the place of Baptism

Mount of Temptation which rises at the back of Jericho.

It was a long but easy ascent, and with every step upward the Jordan Valley looked more terrible in its hot bleached bareness. When I reached the top of this mountain I was still two hundred feet below sea level.

Half-way up, built partly in the rock, I discovered a monastery where ten old Greek monks endure the poverty that has descended on the Eastern Church. Few pilgrims come now to pray in the little grotto where Jesus fasted in the wilderness.

One old man, who could speak two or three words of English, took me over the chapel, with its dust, its dim, gaudy ikons, its unlit candles, and its air of decay and neglect.

He pointed to a cavity beneath an altar, telling me in a solemn low voice that it was the cave in which Jesus slept before He was tempted by the devil. Then he tip-toed off to some other dusty shrine. The air of death about the place, and the old men who tottered about in their black robes, were rather depressing. Then the setting was so improbable and fantastic. A monastery carved out of a mountain side, bits of it built out here and there over ghastly chasms, while other parts of it were cut into the face of the mountain so that the walls and roof were of the rock. I wondered what happened when one of these old

men died. I imagined them cutting a grave in the rock and placing their companion to rest like some ancient Moses on Nebo.

There was something pathetic in their childish pleasure in my visit. The old monk, having shown me the church, led me to a room whose balcony was built out over a sheer drop of more than a thousand feet. The little wooden erection shook so ominously under me that I stepped back into the room. It was a

"There is something slow and gentle and small about the Jordan"

overleaf: near the Dead Sea: "A movement revealed a group of camels, queer prehistoric-looking creatures the very colour of the sandy rocks"

"I was also determined to climb the Mount of Temptation which rises at the back of Jericho" opposite: "He pointed to a cavity beneath an altar, telling me in a solemn low voice that it was the cave in which Jesus slept before He was tempted by the devil"

page 50: "A monastery carved out of a mountain side, bits of it built out here and there over ghastly chasms"

strange little room, furnished according to some dimly remembered standards of the distant earth. A little table with a green cloth occupied the centre, and round the walls were set old horse-hair padded chairs. The only pictures in the room were of the Tzar and the Tzarina, King Tino of Greece and, strangely enough, old-fashioned coloured lithographs of King George and Queen Mary.

The old monk sat with folded hands, smiling affably at me and speaking the most atrocious English.

"Ah!" he said, or rather meant to say, glancing up at the lithograph of the Tzar, "poor, poor Russia!"

He told me that in the old days the mountain path was black with ascending pilgrims from Holy Russia. But now . . . he spread his hands in a gesture of despair. At this point a young monk, the only young one I had seen, entered bearing a tray containing small cups of coffee, little plates of jam and a white liqueur that tasted like absinthe. I drank the coffee and the liqueur and ate the jam, ceremoniously bowing to the old monk from time to time and receiving in return his smiles and bows. The young monk, a rather scared-looking youth in spectacles and with side-whiskers of brown fluff, stood holding the tray and bowing stiffly every time I put back a glass or a plate.

It was the habit in ancient times to treat any stranger as if he might be a wandering Christ, and this beautiful courtesy still exists in out-of-the-way parts of the earth. We have lost it, and with it something fine and beautiful has gone from our lives. When the old monk led me to the main gate and, lifting the latch for me, said good-bye, adding a blessing in Greek, his eyes still held that antique wonder in them. I was a stranger going down and away into mystery. I turned and waved back to him,

and went on down the stony path.

Never shall I forget the sunset flung back upon the hills of Moab, turning them to pink and mauve, filling the gashes in their flanks with dark blue shadows. The brown humped hills lay to the north like a map of the moon, and in the centre of the wilderness I saw the green thread that marks the river whose waters flow to the four corners of Christendom.

Some instinct warned me to stop on the hill that runs up into Nazareth. I looked back to the south over a sweep of country that recalls much of the sorrows and triumphs of a nation.

I saw the great Plain of Esdraelon stretching like a smooth, green sea to the distant hills of Samaria. The shadows of the clouds moved over it as if the ghosts of old armies were crossing the haunted plain. There are over twenty battlefields down there. The level arena has known the thunder of chariots from Egypt, Assyria and Babylon. Somewhere on the plain, Barak smote the Canaanites. From its green levels Gideon drove the Midianites towards the Jordan. On the hills at the back Saul went by night to consult the Witch of Endor, and by day saw his armies scattered and his sons slain. It was down there, too, that the dead body of Josiah was hurried from the triumphant Egyptians and borne in sorrow to Jerusalem.

The brown hills to the south, the hills of Samaria, had known the denunciatory figure of Elijah. They had heard his burning words and seen the prophetic fire in his eyes. On the skyline was the hill that held Naboth's Vineyard and the hill on which Jezebel met death. To the right the long calm ridge of Carmel cut the sky, and I looked at it remembering the priests of Baal and the fire that Elijah drew down from heaven to confound them.

When I had looked my fill at this tremendous map of Old Testament history, I went on through Nazareth; and the road ran upward to the top of another hill. There I stopped, not from instinct but from amazement; for down below me to the northward lay a new world—Galilee.

I do not know the name of this hill, but I shall always think of it as the Hill of the Two Testaments.

To the south lies the Old Testament; to the north lie Galilee and the New. As I looked northward to the new land, the idea came to me that this hill reproduces in nature the title-page which printers of the Bible place between the books of the prophets and the life of Christ. And I thought that although Jesus may not have visited all the places which are now called holy, there can be no doubt that He must have often stood on this hill as a boy. He must have

Old Jericho – "There is
nothing to-day but a
huge mound of sun-
caked earth from which
the point of a stick will
turn up fragments of
ancient pottery"
overleaf: "The green-
ness of Jericho rose up,
an oasis in the dreadful
desolation"

Beersheba market

left: "Here and there the desolation was broken by a few tethered horses, a few she-camels and their long-legged infants, and perhaps a flock of sheep nosing the burning earth for stray grass"

known all His nation's ghosts, which crowd up from the south, and He must have looked with affection towards the calm and lovely north and the road that runs down over the mountains to the lake.

One pictures Him in imagination rising from the hill as the sun drops into the sea and going down through the hush of the twilight to Nazareth. Night is closing in on the Plain of Esdraelon and the hills of Samaria are already in shadow. But the last thing that fades from sight on the plain below is a white streak. It is the road that goes on through Samaria and through the wilderness of Judaea to end at last far to the south before the gates of Jerusalem.

As I went down into Galilee, I knew that I had learnt something about the Gospels that I could never have known in any other way. Nazareth is a frontier post between the north and the south. To go into Galilee is to turn one's back on the arena of the Old Testament, and there is something in the formation of the land that gives a feeling of finality to the act: one cannot possibly go into Galilee without the knowledge that one has definitely said farewell to Judaea. It is not until one crosses this Hill of the Two Testaments that one's mind shakes itself free from the powerful hypnotism of Jerusalem.

By going into Galilee Jesus performed a symbolic act. He turned His back on the world of the Old Testament, and from the moment of that turning away the New Testament begins.

Everyone must feel how different are these two worlds. In the New Testament we seem to have emerged from a dark, fierce Eastern world into a clear light that is almost European. In fact Rome is

The Church of the
Loaves and Fishes, by
the Sea of Galilee

above right and overleaf:
The Sea of Galilee,
"even in its desolation,
breathes an exquisite
peace and a beauty that
surpasses anything in
the Holy Land"

Damascus, or a Greek architect on his way to build a new theatre in Jerash in the Decapolis.

This busy international corridor was the place in which Jesus taught. He alone of all the prophets who had come out of Israel deliberately cut Himself off from the theological stronghold of Judaea. And the roads He chose to tread were not the roads of the priests and the rabbis but the roads of the world. So in the road that runs over a hill from Nazareth to the Sea of Galilee a man detects the first promise of Christianity.

The little hotel in Tiberias stands near the lake. From my room I could see over the flat roofs of houses and, through the branches of eucalyptus trees, a strip of blue water backed by a range of hills as barren and as pink and mauve in colour as the Mountains of Moab at Jericho. The room was hot and stuffy, but, unlike the dry, windless heat of the Dead Sea, it was tempered by a slight breeze from the lake, a breeze not strong enough to move the palm fronds but enough to shake the eucalyptus leaves.

I have discovered that whenever one arrives in an hotel in the land it is a good idea to follow the stairs right to the top. There is always a flat roof that gives an excellent general view of whatever town one may happen to be in. I came out on a space as large as a tennis-court, so white and dazzling that I could see nothing until I had put on sun glasses. Then I looked down on Tiberias.

I saw hundreds of flat-roofed white houses marching down a gentle hill-slope to stand in picturesque confusion on the lake-side. Little white domes varied the rectangular uniformity of the white roofs. Here and there a minaret like a Georgian pepper-pot stood up higher than domes or roofs. There was one dark, narrow main street from which hundreds of squalid little lanes radiated, and this street was congested with men, women, children, camels and donkeys. The background was a high green mountain with a few houses dotted about its slopes.

In front of me the Sea of Galilee lay ruffled by a slight wind. It was not a uniform colour. There were patches of dark and light blue and also touches of pale green. I wondered with what lake I could

already in sight. The centre of the Old Testament world is rigid, exclusive Jerusalem; the centre of the New Testament world is international Galilee, a country crossed in the time of Christ by the great military roads from the north and by the ancient caravan routes from the east, a country in which a man seen in the distance might be an imperial messenger riding to Caesarea with tidings of the Emperor's death, or a tax-gatherer from the main road to

compare it, and explored my memory in vain. The Emperor Titus intended to call the Lake of Neuchâtel, in Switzerland, Galilaea because it reminded him so much of the Sea of Galilee, but he must have changed his mind. The lake is heart-shaped, with the narrowest part to the south. It is thirteen miles long and at its widest part about seven miles across. Mountains rise all round the lake. On the western shore they are green mountains; on the eastern shore they are the brown barren precipices of the desert, part of the rocky barrier that rises east of the Jordan and marches south with the river, past the Dead Sea down to the Gulf of Akaba. When I looked to the north I saw the sight that impresses itself upon the mind of all who live in Galilee: I saw a magnificent ridge of mountain covered with snow. It stood up like a screen to the north. The snow never melts in its deepest corries even in the height of summer. It was Mount Hermon, the Mountain of the Transfiguration.

What makes it so impossible to compare the Sea of Galilee with any European lake is the sub-tropical climate. It is a little inland sea sunk at the beginning of the tropical trench that divides Palestine from Arabia. It is seven hundred feet below sea level and, like its companion lake, the Dead Sea, many miles due south, it belongs to a different latitude from the rest of the land. The mountains that rise all round it have their heads in a temperate climate and their feet in a lake round whose shores banana, palm, bamboo and sugarcane thrive. And the water of the Sea of Galilee is fresh, not·salt and bitter like that of the Dead Sea.

The second thing that impresses one about the Sea of Galilee is its desolation. It is, with the exception of the white town of Tiberias, a deserted lake. Through glasses one can see, far off along the western bank towards the north, a dark clump of eucalyptus trees which are supposed to mark the site of Bethsaida, and next to them a small white building and more trees which stand where Capernaum is believed to have stood. You see uneasy mounds of black stones near the shore which are the dead bones of old cities. When you look at the pink and mauve hills opposite, you see that they are wild and desolate, slashed with brown thirsty valleys as with the slashes of knives. Dotted about them here and there are little black squares, sometimes near the shore but more often higher on the hills. They are the goat-hair tents of Bedouin tribes. There are few roads. Mud villages are mounted on the tops of mountains, and the traveller who ventures among them without a knowledge of the language is advised to take an armed escort with him.

But the Sea of Galilee, even in its desolation, breathes an exquisite peace and a beauty that surpass anything in the land. The landscape has altered in detail since Jesus made His home in Capernaum, but the broad outline has not changed. The hills are the hills He looked upon, the lights and shadows that turn the Gergesene heights to gold and purple, the little breezes that whip the lake into whiteness, the blue water that fades to a milky green where the Jordan enters at the north; none of these has changed. These are the things that Jesus looked upon and loved when He lived in Galilee.

I took the boat one morning and rowed among the lonely little bays to the north of Tabgha. It was a perfect day and I had not seen the lake a deeper blue. The bare hills rose from the water to lie in gentle curves against the sky. Piles of black basalt lay everywhere, on the hills and at the water's edge, and so characteristic is this volcanic stone that even the lizards have coloured themselves in imitation of it. In the curve of a small bay a white temple hides itself

pages 68-9: *Capernaum*

"*One comes across Jerash delighted and astonished to find that while Gaza, Ascalon, Caesarea Philippi, and other Roman cities have fallen into dust, this one at least remains with its pavements, its baths, the ruins of its temples, its theatres, its forum and its houses*"

with a withered hand. If not from this bay, from one exactly like it, Jesus put out in a little boat and spoke to the multitudes that were gathered on the shore.

This white ruin among the eucalyptus grove is, I think, one of the most touching links with our Lord's Ministry to be seen in the Holy Land. The Franciscan friars, who guard each stone with love and reverence, have left untouched this white ruin facing the lake, so that one can sit there and know that Jesus, when He stood there, looked across the blue water to the parched hills of "the desert place" opposite, and saw, to the south, the lake stretching into a heat haze that gives an illusion of the sea.

The synagogue must have been one of the most beautiful in Galilee and the frequency with which it occurs in the Gospel story suggests that it was possibly the most important one on the lakeside. Perhaps the Bedouin strain in the Jews explains why they never developed an architecture of their own. Even their chief building, the Temple in Jerusalem, was a modification, first of Phoenician and, later, of Greek architecture. And this temple by the lake is plainly Roman. That is one reason why many learned scholars have suggested that it was built in the time of Christ by the Good Centurion of Capernaum. You remember how St. Luke tells that when the centurion's servant fell ill the elders of the Jews went to Jesus, saying that the Centurion was worthy of help because "he loveth our nation and hath built us a synagogue."

among hedges and eucalyptus trees. There are four columns upholding a broken architrave, a paved court in which the grass grows, a doorway that leads nowhere, and the usual chaos of broken pillars and fallen stones. Most scholars now agree that this is all that is left of Capernaum.

I tied up the boat and, walking through the garden of the Franciscan friars, who have their dwelling near by, wandered among the tumbled stones. The temple is the ruin of Capernaum's synagogue. Some experts say that it is the very building in which Jesus preached and performed His miracles; others say that it is not actually the building, but one erected much later on the same spot. But does it matter? It was here that Jesus Christ lived during the two or three most important years in the world's history. Somewhere among the piles of black basalt that scatter the hillocks is the site of Peter's house, where our Lord lived; somewhere on the little curve of shore is the very spot where "he saw Simon and Andrew, his brother, casting a net into the sea: for they were fishers. And Jesus said unto them, 'Come ye after me and I will make you to become fishers of men.'" A little further along the shore is the place where James and John, the sons of Zebedee, left their father in the boat with the hired servants in order to follow the Master. Perhaps on this very spot, deserted now except by the little black lizards that run among the stones, Jesus expelled the unclean spirit and healed the man

I went on to the south until I came to the melancholy desolation that was Caesarea. During the lifetime of Jesus this was a port as large as the Piraeus. Its harbour, its buildings and its fine streets were famous among the world's seaports. Herod, who began to build it in 25 B.C. and took twelve years to finish it, employed the finest architects of the time and the most up-to-date engineers, so that Caesarea ranked among the ancient towns of the Holy Land like a small New York. All the streets led to the harbour and were intersected by straight parallel avenues. We would probably have considered it the best type of American city! The remains of subways which connected various parts of the city with the beach have also been discovered. There were magnificent theatres and a hippodrome, and facing the sea was the marble temple which Herod built to the honour of his master, Caesar.

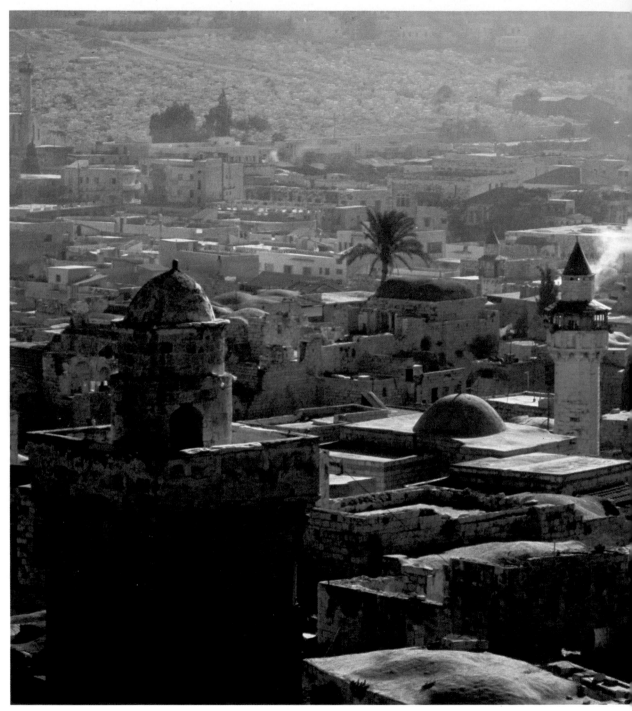

"The busy streets of Nablus (the Shechem of Genesis) are narrow dark tunnels crowded with camels, donkeys, and the vivid life of the East"

pages 72-3: Fields near Jerusalem

and in Caesarea the legions hailed Vespasian as their emperor.

And to-day there is nothing. The sea beats on a desolate coast. There is a rock some way out at sea which may be a relic of the once famous harbour, and the palace in which Pilate lived, the splendid forum, the great hippodrome, and the circus, are now meagre cornfields.

On the roads of the Holy Land, and on the hills, you see the good shepherd. He comes along at the head of his flock, generally carrying over his shoulders a lamb or an injured sheep.

He is a man burnt almost black by exposure to the sun. He wears the flowing Bedouin head-veil, the *keffiyeh*, bound with two black twisted cords known as the *agaal*. Beneath his robes he often wears a sheepskin coat with the fleece turned next to the body. He is one of the many characters who walk the roads of the Holy Land exactly as they must have done in the time or our Lord.

A most remarkable thing is the sympathy that exists between him and his flock. He never drives them as our own shepherds drive their sheep. He always walks at their head, leading them along the roads and over the hills to new pasture: and, as he goes, he sometimes talks to them in a loud sing-song voice, using a weird language unlike anything I have

One can imagine how readily the Romans centred their authority in this splendid modern seaport and how glad Pilate must have been to have lived there in the great palace of Herod rather than in the old and savage city of Jerusalem. It was from Caesarea that Pilate set out with his retinue to attend the Passover during which he condemned Jesus to the cross; it was to Caesarea that St. Paul came many times, once under escort after his arrest in Jerusalem;

"It is a road whose
serpentine bends and
overhanging cliffs might
have been designed for
highway robbery"

words were animal sounds arranged in a kind of order. No sooner had he spoken than an answering bleat shivered over the herd, and one or two of the animals turned their heads in his direction. But they did not obey him. The goat-herd then called out one word and gave a laughing kind of whinny. Immediately a goat with a bell round his neck stopped eating and, leaving the herd, trotted down the hill, across the valley and up the opposite slopes. The man, accompanied by this animal, walked on and disappeared round a ledge of rock. Very soon a panic spread among the herd. They forgot to eat. They looked up for the shepherd. He was not to be seen. They became conscious that the leader with the bell at his neck was no longer with them. From the distance came the strange laughing call of the shepherd, and at the sound of it the entire herd stampeded into the hollow and leapt up the hill after him.

I would like to know what an English sheep-dog would make of the sheep of the Holy Land, because our principle of droving is something that neither Arab shepherds nor their sheep-dogs understand. It is all done by word of mouth, and the sheep follow their shepherds like dogs. The Arab sheep-dog is used therefore not to drive sheep but to protect them against thieves and wild animals.

Early one morning I saw an extraordinary sight not far from Bethlehem. Two shepherds had evidently spent the night with their flocks in a cave. The sheep were all mixed together and the time had come for the shepherds to go in different directions. One of the shepherds stood some distance from the sheep and began to call. First one, then another, then four or five animals ran towards him; and so on until he had counted his whole flock.

More interesting than the sight of this was the knowledge that Jesus must have seen exactly the same sight and described it in His own words:

"He calleth his own sheep by name, and leadeth them out. And when he putteth forth his own sheep, he goeth before them, and the sheep follow him: for they know his voice. And a stranger they will not follow, but will flee from him: for they know not the voice of strangers. This parable spake Jesus unto them. . . . I am the good shepherd, and know my sheep and am known of mine."

ever heard in my life. The first time I heard this sheep and goat language I was on the hills at the back of Jericho. A goat-herd had descended into a valley and was mounting the slope of an opposite hill when, turning round, he saw his goats had remained behind to devour a rich patch of scrub. Lifting his voice, he spoke to the goats in a language that Pan must have spoken on the mountains of Greece. It was uncanny because there was nothing human about it. The

Triumph and Trial

Jerusalem

following pages:
Jerusalem, the Golden
Gate
The Damascus Gate

WHEN JESUS SAYS good-bye to Galilee and turns His steps towards Jerusalem, a tenseness creeps into the Gospel narrative. The lovely idyll of Galilee is over. Never again do we hear the waves falling on the lakeside, or watch a great crowd settling on the grass, or see the little fishing-boats come swinging home against the sunset. Jerusalem, high and cold on its hill, terrifying in its formalism and self-conceit, its arrogance and its supreme blindness, lies like a storm-cloud in the path of Christ.

With a wonderful economy of words the Gospels succeed in suggesting the atmosphere of the city, like the first roll of thunder on the wings of an approaching storm. Jerusalem stretches out tentacles to trap Him. Spies waylay Him to ensnare Him in rabbinical argument. He waves them off with cold, icy logic, and passes on His way out of the hot valley of the Jordan to the high, brown mountains and the storm. Never before have violence, great crowds, rings of heated faces, accusing fingers, lying enemies and the feeling of a city in the grip of fanatical hatred been suggested in fewer words. Classical literature contains nothing so vivid as the Gospel account of the events that led to the Crucifixion, and, as we read them, the background, never described but always suggested, is the tense, nervous atmosphere of Jerusalem.

It is an extraordinary thing that this atmosphere is characteristic of Jerusalem to-day. The city has been destroyed many times, but each time it has risen from the dead the same nervous, tense Jerusalem. The tightness in the air is a strange impalpable thing, but so real that it is a relief to escape beyond the walls of the city, if it is only as far as the Mount of Olives. No sooner do you return and pass in under one of the old gates, than you fall again under the influence of this strange power.

In the old days the electricity in the air of Jerusalem was due to the Temple and everything that the rigid Temple worship stood for in the life of Judaism; to-day it is due to the fact that the Holy City has become a thrice-holy city, and that within its walls three great faiths are always in danger of conflict. The Christian, who naturally regards Jerusalem only as the scene of the Crucifixion and the Resurrection, is apt to forget that to the Jew it is still the city of Jehovah, and to the Moslem it is the most sacred spot on earth outside Mecca. The threshing-floor of Ornan the Jebusite, which became the altar of burnt offerings in the Temple of Solomon, is to-day a Moslem shrine and from this rock, so the Moslems believe, the Prophet ascended into heaven on the back of his winged steed, el-Barûk.

It is therefore not difficult to understand why Jerusalem is filled with a violence of mind instead of the violence of physical action which characterises all modern cities. It would be unwise for a Jew to enter the Holy Sepulchre, and the great mosque is often closed to Christians. The air is full of a feeling of spiritual barriers and frontiers. Nothing matters in Jerusalem but religion. Although it is one of the most polyglot cities on earth, there are no national-

ities. A man is seldom referred to as a Swiss, a German, an Armenian, a Persian, a Copt, or a Greek: he is either a Christian, a Moslem, or a Jew. These three faiths are to Jerusalem what nationality is to other cities.

It is not, perhaps, surprising that three conflicting ideas about Eternity should result in a general disagreement about time. Christian, Moslem and Jew live in different years. With us it is 1934 A.D. The Jews, however, counting from the creation of the world, estimate the date as 5694. The Moslems, counting from the birth of Mahomet, make it 1352. But there is even a fourth time-table, that of the Greeks and Russians, who employ the obsolete Julian Calendar, which was devised by Julius Caesar in 46 B.C. and corrected by Pope Gregory XIII in 1582.

Then Jerusalem has three holy days every week. The Moslems revere Friday, the Jews keep Saturday sacred, and the Christians follow on with their Sunday. A delightfully bizarre touch is given to Jerusalem by the Abyssinian Christians, who celebrate Christmas once a month; but that, fortunately, is purely a private affair, and does not close the banks. In this chaos of sacred observance the life of a bank clerk in Jerusalem must be at least half-way to heaven, because at Easter time Mr. Barclay almost ceases to function. Holy days succeed one another for nearly a week, and Mr. Barclay draws his blinds reverently for the Passover, for Nebi Musa, and for Easter.

So Jerusalem expresses in her daily life the complexity of all great junctions. Three main lines of faith meet there in apparent confusion before spreading out to the ends of the earth.

I went to an hotel not far from the Jaffa Gate where an Arab, who was dressed like a Turk in a musical comedy, carried up my bags. An Armenian registered me. A German chambermaid unlocked my bedroom door.

It was an attractive room with a writing-table and a good light over the bed, and it had a little balcony overlooking a narrow street and the walls of a convent school. Through the windows I could see the nuns moving about a large, bare dormitory, making two rows of little beds.

I went straight out to find my way to the Church of the Holy Sepulchre. I had been studying a street plan of Jerusalem for weeks, and wondered whether I could find my way alone through the twisting lanes of the old city. As soon as I appeared in the Jaffa Road I was surrounded by eager, whispering men, wearing European suits and the red tarbush which used to be the sign of Turkish citizenship.

"You come with me to the Holy Sepulchre!" they whispered. "I show you everything!"

There seemed to me to be a definite blasphemy in their invitations, so I shook them off and went on alone. They followed me like figures in a nightmare, whispering, and once even daring to pull me by the

sleeve. I had to make it very clear that I disliked them before they disappeared from sight. I was distressed to find that the real Jerusalem, full of donkeys and camels and men selling oranges, was very different from the clear street plan that I knew by heart! I came to the Jaffa Gate and saw a great sweep of the city wall running to the south. I passed in and entered the old city. I saw to my right the huge, square tower, known as David's Tower, which is in reality all that is left of Herod's great tower, Phasael. I saw it with the emotion which any relic of the time of Christ must inspire, whether the observer be a devout Christian or merely a devout historian. Those huge yellow stones at the base of the tower existed in the Jerusalem of the Crucifixion. Perhaps His eyes saw them.

Round this tower and near the Gate surged an extraordinary crowd, which seemed to me, so newly from the West, to be a perfect microcosm of the East, and I looked at it with the delight of a child at a Christmas circus.

I could distinguish peasants from the villages, the *fellahin*, born farmers and ploughmen, who are a queer mixture of cunning, simplicity and violence. Then, quite distinct from the *fellah*, was the Bedouin Arab. Although he walked in rags, he moved like a king of the earth. He despises the *fellah* and his spade. The Bedouin is a man of ancestry and freedom, of flocks and herds, and tents which he calls "houses of hair." In him Abraham lives on into the modern world.

There were the town Arabs in European clothes and tarbushes. There were Armenians, Franciscan friars, and white Dominicans. There were Greek priests, who are square-bearded like Assyrian kings and stride through the crowd wearing rusty cassocks and high round black hats. Strangest of all were the old Jews with their long, straggling beards, and curls of hair tapping against their temples. These Ashkenazim Jews, wearing velvet gabardines and large, fur-rimmed hats, moved through the crowd, in it but not of it, silently, and, it seemed, timidly, unreadable men locked away in the mysterious depths of their own spiritual history. There were the Sephardic Jews, also Orthodox, who wore low, wide-rimmed black felt hats, and many of them were pale, spectacled and peering, with thin, fair beards.

The Oriental possesses the gift of intense passion and of an equally intense lassitude. Arabs sat dreamily under the awning of a café, sucking at hookahs; others, strung up to a high pitch of excitement, expended in the purchase of a handful of dates, or a lettuce, more passion than a Westerner expends in a month.

I dived into David Street, which leads down towards the Church of the Holy Sepulchre. This street is typical of the lanes of old Jerusalem, which no motor traffic can ever invade. It descends in a series of steps, with a line of booths on each side. It is so narrow, and so packed with people of all kinds, of all ages and of all sizes, that you often stand helplessly with a donkey's head over your shoulder and a sack

of millet against your face. There is nothing to do but to wait cheerfully and hope that those who are holding up the procession will move on. David Street is dark and cool. Sometimes the sun, slanting down into its depths, falls in a dazzling pool on a pile of oranges, melons, cucumbers and artichokes, or on a pile of the least edible looking fish you can imagine, or, more pleasantly, upon a rotund collarless person who, sitting behind a chromatic barricade of Syrian silk, every now and then lifts to his mouth a brown, ringed hand holding a gold-tipped cigarette.

In spite of all my maps and plans I confessed myself hopelessly lost in this bright chaos, but I walked on with resolution, knowing that if I appeared to hesitate for one instant a pack of guides would be on my heels. But it was not a pleasant feeling because, when I had left the crowd behind, I found myself in dark, narrow lanes faced with scabrous walls, broken only by dark openings to cellars or to dank little courtyards into which cats darted with the speed and terror of wild animals. The thought crossed my mind that anyone who ventures alone into these lanes without a knowledge of Arabic deserves a knife in the back.

I went into one of the antique shops near the Jaffa Gate. I do not know why one buys bits of gangrened bronze, coins, fragments of iridescent glass, bone pins, old mirrors, and all the odd scraps which someone flung on a rubbish-heap centuries ago, unless, perhaps, one feels that they possess, or should possess, the power of association. I have been collecting such trifles since I was a boy at school, because I like to hold them and to think "When this was new Cleopatra had not yet met Antony and the Battle of Actium was still far off," or, "When this green wire was a brooch St. Paul was just setting off on his first missionary journey." It is the most harmless form of speculation in the world. It is, however, sometimes haunted by the laughter of the dead, for what could seem more ludicrous to the shade of a Roman matron than the sight of someone mounting her old saucepan handle against a background of black velvet?

The merchant had a fine selection of Roman glass, bronze pots, copper and bronze daggers, and some exquisite bronze incense shovels found, so I was told, on the mounds near a Roman city in the desert. I bought two incense shovels and, while poking about in a drawer full of scraps, discovered a Roman tile embossed with a circular stamp and the letters "Leg.X.F." On the top of the stamp was a rough impression of a galley and beneath the letters was an animal that looked like a pig or a boar. I could hardly believe my eyes.

"Do you know what this is?" I asked the merchant.

"Yes," he replied, "it is a tile with the stamp of the Tenth Legion on it. They are often found in Jerusalem. You can have it for five shillings."

I gave him the trifle and went away more pleased with the tile than with my expensive incense shovels,

for I had in my pocket a relic of the legion that, in destroying Jerusalem under Titus in 70 A.D., fulfilled the prophesy of Christ that there should not be one stone of the Temple left upon another.

I took the tile to my bathroom, where I sponged it. It was covered with a hard incrustation of brown soil, which yielded eventually to moisture and came off leaving the "Leg.X.F." slightly clearer and exposing the legionary badge of the galley and the boar. I must admit, however, that neither of these symbols would have been recognisable to anyone who did not know what to look for. The Tenth Legion, which had made this tile about forty years after the Crucifixion, was known as the "Fretensis"—the legion from "fretum Siciliense," the Straits of Sicily—and the letter F. was the initial of the word "Fretensis." As I dried the legionary tile, and felt it hard under my hands, I longed to be able by some process of clairvoyance to see the world of which it was so provoking a fragment. . . .

As the sun sets behind Jerusalem on a Friday night, a hush falls over the Jewish quarter. The Sabbath has begun.

The warren of small houses in the network of narrow streets has been washed clean. You look through archways into small yards scrubbed white. Pots and pans have been scoured. Sabbath lamps are lit. And through the streets of the old city pass some of the strangest and most picturesque figures in the world to-day: patriarchs in velvet gabardines and round, fur-rimmed hats; pallid, sandy-haired young Jews with fanatical eyes and long hair, two corkscrew curls falling from their temples on each side and tapping against their cheeks; and little boys in their Sabbath garments, leading by the hand some tottering ancient, grown old and kind.

These are the old-fashioned Orthodox Jews, who live according to the Law of Moses, who weep at the Wailing Wall for the lost glories of Israel, and whose lives are rigidly bound by the minute prohibitions of the Mosaic law.

Their settlement in Jerusalem is recent, as dates go in the ancient city. The Crusaders massacred every Jew and Jewess when they captured Jerusalem. It was not until the Arab conquest and the European persecution of the Jews during the Middle Ages that small groups began to trickle back.

This strange community contains to-day a number of interesting sects. There are Sephardic Jews, who came originally from Spain, Morocco and Algeria, in 1492. They speak Ladino, a kind of broken Castilian. There are the Ashkenazim, from Central and Eastern Europe. There are picturesque Bokhara Jews from Persia, and Jews from Samarkand, who speak a Persian Yiddish.

An extraordinary people are the Yemenites, who arrived during the last century from the wilds of Arabia, claiming to be the tribe of Gad, and speaking both Hebrew and Arabic.

There are the Qaarites, who live under a curse, and

the Hassidic Jews, who dance like dervishes in their synagogue. There are also the fanatical fur-hatted Jews with ear-curls, known as Agudath Israel. They talk Yiddish and refuse to speak Hebrew because they believe that its use in ordinary life is a blasphemy. They spend their time poring over the sacred books. When the Sabbath begins on Friday night, they turn out to see that all the Jewish shops are shut. If any are open, they picket the doors.

Early one Sabbath morning a young Jew took me round the synagogues in the old city. It was extraordinarily interesting. We plunged straight into the Old Testament. The narrow streets and the labyrinth of houses are full of synagogues, often merely a small room containing a few books on shelves or cupboards, a tribune, and a reading-desk containing the Torah, or Pentateuch, written on parchment and fixed to rollers.

Ancient Jews, with spectacles on the tips of their noses, rocked themselves backwards and forwards as they recited prayers; little boys and young men kept up a perpetual swaying and muttering as they repeated the sacred words.

In a synagogue of Moroccan Jews the congregation sat on the floor like Moors and the women were hidden, like wives in a harem, behind an openwork screen.

In nearly all these synagogues I saw something that illuminated a passage in St. Luke: the story of Jesus as a child of twelve disputing with the rabbis in the Temple. There were small boys in their Sabbath clothes, prayer-rugs over their shoulders, sitting beside their fathers or their grandfathers, and carefully applying themselves to the Law, repeating the words in monotonous voices and rocking their small bodies.

In one obscure synagogue, I think of Ashkenazim Jews, the morning service had just ended. A lad of about twelve years of age was standing before three bearded elders, talking to them in a precocious and animated manner. Sometimes he pleased them, and they smiled and patted him on the shoulder; but

"So Jerusalem expresses in her daily life the complexity of all great junctions. The three main lines of faith meet there in apparent confusion before spreading out to the ends of the earth"

sometimes he annoyed them, and the three old men shook their beards in disagreement and frowned at the lad over their spectacles. But the little fellow stood his ground, waiting respectfully to be spoken to; then, his questions over, he gave a little bob to the old men and walked slowly away.

This, I thought, must have been something like the sight that met the eyes of Joseph and Mary when, seeking Jesus, "they found Him in the Temple, sitting in the midst of the doctors, both hearing them and asking them questions."

We found our way to the Wailing Wall down narrow winding lanes in the old city. Turning a corner suddenly, we came upon an enormous tawny stretch of wall from whose cracks grow tufts of grass and wild caper plants. The wall is about fifty yards long and sixty feet high, and the lower courses are of enormous blocks of brownish stone—one of sixteen and a half feet long and thirteen feet wide. This is believed to be the only fragment of the Temple wall which the soldiers of Titus did not destroy after the siege.

The custom of wailing, or mourning, is one that occurs frequently in the Old Testament.

"Therefore I will wail and howl," cried Micah the Morasthite. "I will go stripped and naked: I will make a wailing like the dragons and mourning as the owls."

"We grope for the wall like the blind," says Isaiah, "and we grope as if we had no eyes: we stumble at noonday as in the night; we are in desolate places as dead men. We roar all like bears, and mourn sore like doves. . . ."

The custom of wailing at the wall of Herod's Temple goes back to remote times. After the destruction of Jerusalem, Hadrian forbade Jews even to come within sight of the city, on pain of death. Under Constantine, however, they were allowed to weep on the site of the Temple once a year. In the twelfth century the exterior wall—the present Wailing Wall —was allotted to the Jews as a place for prayer.

About fifty Jews, men and women, were standing against the wall, some with books, and all of them muttering swiftly as they rocked their bodies to and fro, as Jews always do when they pray.

Many types of Jew come down to the Wailing Wall. I saw the Polish Jew in his velvet gabardine and his fur-rimmed hat, young Jews with long, sandy hair and side-curls, dark Eastern Jews, Yemenites from Arabia, who look exactly like Arabs, Spanish Jews, and, here and there, a modern Jew in a lounge suit and a cap.

Little prayers, written on scraps of paper, were stuck in the cracks of the stones. One girl wept bitterly as she rocked herself beside the wall, praying perhaps for the recovery of someone from illness, for the Jews believe that Jehovah has never deserted or withdrawn His compassion from those stones. Prayers from Jews all over the world were, and probably are still, offered up at the Wailing Wall in

left: At the Wailing Wall

below: Bethlehem – "Above the flat, white roofs rise the bell-towers of convents and orphanages and monasteries. There is always a bell ringing in the heat"

order to gain the privilege of the special sanctity which attaches itself to the wall.

Many of the "wailers" joined in regular litanies. This is one of them, which the young Zionist translated for me:

Leader: For the palace that lies desolate.
Response: We sit in solitude and mourn.
Leader: For the Temple that is destroyed.
Response: We sit in solitude and mourn.
Leader: For the walls that are overthrown.
Response: We sit in solitude and mourn.
Leader: For our majesty that is departed.
Response: We sit in solitude and mourn.

This, I suppose, is the lamentation that has been in the heart of the Orthodox Jew since Titus destroyed the Temple of Herod and scattered the race to the four corners of the world.

The sun has not yet risen. Sleepy donkeys are being led through the streets of Jerusalem. Camels in long files are plodding in from the villages with greenstuff. Bundles of rags, lying on the ledges and under the arches of the Damascus Gate, stir and stretch out lean, brown arms.

In the steep streets of the old city the fruiterers are setting out their bright stalls, cloth merchants are busy with their bales, pastry-cooks are already mak-

ing their small sugary cakes; and fish merchants are putting out the queer, misshapen corpses which are sold and eaten in this mountain capital, huge pike from the Tigris and the Euphrates, which come overland in four days packed in ice, flat fish from Egypt and Jaffa, and the *musht*, a grayling known as St. Peter's fish, which is caught only in the Lake of Galilee.

As I go down the terraced streets, beautifully cool

These and the following pages show how traditional and modern ways of life walk hand in hand — in Jerusalem and outside

War and poverty, grim realities in the Sinai desert (left) and near the Damascus Gate (above) overleaf: peace outside Jerusalem

91

ק ברקליס
ISCOUNT BANI

in the morning air, ancient, gloomy walls rise up on each side, and I come upon a crusaders' arch, now built into the wall of a mosque, or a blue-tiled fountain built in the time of Saladin. Suddenly the dark little street is filled with a tawny brilliance, and, glancing up, I know that the sun has risen. I can already feel the warmth in the air, for the sun in Palestine leaps up into the sky like a ball of fire and is warm to the skin from the first second of his arrival.

I hear the call to prayer from the nearest minaret. As I turn the corner, I see the muezzin standing in his little railed-in balcony, lit by the first light of the sun, an old blind man who cries in a loud chanting voice: "Allâhu akbar, Allâhu akbar. Allâhu akbar; ashadu an lâ ilâha illa-llâh, ashadu anna Muhammedarrasûlullâh . . . hayya 'alas-salâ . . . Allah is great; testify that there is no God but Allah and Mohammed is his Prophet . . . Come to prayer!"

And as he calls he does not cup his hands to his mouth, as artists always paint him, but he holds them behind his ears, the palms to the front and the fingers up.

I go on over the rough cobbles and, passing through the Gate of St. Stephen, I see ahead of me a blinding sandy road and the Mount of Olives with the sun above it.

In mountain country there is nothing older than a road. Cities may come and go, the most splendid buildings may live and die, but the little road that runs between the rocks lives for ever. One is shown all kinds of sites in Jerusalem which may be open to doubt—such as the very spot on which the cock crowed when St. Peter denied his Lord—but one looks at them with respect for the piety which created them, and with distaste for the principle which profits from them. On the Mount of Olives, however, one *knows* that these little stony tracks that twist and turn over the rocks are the very paths that He must have taken and that they are marked more truly with the imprint of His feet than any rock within a golden shrine.

The road runs downhill from St. Stephen's Gate into the Kedron Valley. It bends to the right, leading down to the stony place, and, when I look up, the walls of Jerusalem, with their crenellated sentry-walks, stand like a challenge, golden in the morning sun. At the bottom of the valley the road rises over the lower slopes of the Mount of Olives, and a little to the right stands a clump of cypress trees with a wall round them. This is the Garden of Gethsemane.

The Franciscan friars, who touch everything with beauty, grace and reverence, own the little Garden and, while they have built a church near by, they have not touched the Garden except to make flower-beds among the ancient olive trees.

In a land where the footsteps of Christ, real or imaginary, can be traced by huge churches built over stones and caves and legends, this quiet little Garden on the Mount of Olives stands out as an imperishable memory. Time has not altered this Garden. City has followed city on the hill opposite, but the Garden,

so near that in the evening the shadow of Jerusalem's wall falls across it, has remained to-day as it must have been in the time of Jesus. There would have been a wall round it and probably an oil press to which the people on the Mount would have carried their olives to be crushed. Dotted about the garden are eight aged olive trees of tremendous girth. They are more like rocks than trees. Slim new shoots spring out of apparently dead wood, and the old trunks, vast as ancient oaks, are propped up with ramparts of stones and stout wooden poles. These trees still bear fruit from which the monks press oil.

An old monk, who is working in the Garden, unlocks the gate for me and turns again to his weeding basket and his rake.

He is a French monk who has spent many years in the Holy Land, and when I talk to him he straightens himself from the hedge of rosemary and stands, politely anxious to get on with his work, his brown gardener's hands folded across his brown habit, the fingers locked together.

He points out to me a rock which marks the place where Peter, James and John slept, and not far off is a column in the wall which is the traditional spot on which Judas betrayed Jesus with a kiss.

"And is it true," I ask him, "as so many believe, that these are the actual trees that were growing in the time of Our Lord?"

"They may well be the trees," he replies, "for their age is lost in antiquity. I will tell you a very interest-

While shepherds still watch their flocks near Beersheba (left), modern agriculture brings in the artichokes on a kibbutz

The refugee camp near Jericho (below) is deserted, but the narrow streets of old Jerusalem are bustling with activity

ing thing about them. They have never paid the tax which, since the Moslem conquest, was imposed on newly planted trees. That means that they were not young trees many centuries ago. That, my son, is an historic fact, but whether they sheltered our Lord I cannot say; but, for myself," and here the old man smiled gently and bent towards his rake and basket, "I believe they did."

I looked up and read on a blue plate let into the wall, *Via Dolorosa*.

"If I follow this," I thought, "it is bound to lead me to Calvary, which is inside the Holy Sepulchre."

And no sooner had I thought it than I felt ashamed of my thought. I had blundered on the Way of the Cross and I had treated it as if it were any ordinary street. I felt ill at ease. I set this down because it is so typical of one's first thoughts in Jerusalem. The mind, accustomed to the divine Christ of Western churches, encounters in Jerusalem the memory of Jesus the Man, the Jesus who ate and slept and became weary, who drove the hucksters from the Temple, who drank the cup of death on Golgotha. At home one always thinks of Jesus in heaven, on the right hand of God the Father, but in Jerusalem one thinks of Him walking the dusty white roads, and one's intelligence is perpetually rejecting or accepting certain places that tradition associates with His manhood. As God, He is everywhere, but in Jerusalem

centuries of piety have competed to place His footsteps on this stone and that road. It was almost with a shock that I realised that the *Via Dolorosa* could be a real road with men and women and animals upon it.

I do not know for certain whether the *Via Dolorosa* is really the road on which Jesus carried the Cross, and neither, I think, does anyone else. Its route depends on the situation of Pilate's judgment hall and the unknown position of the Gate Genath. But it does not seem to me to matter very much whether it is the actual road or a memorial to the actual road. What is important is that men and women who have walked upon it have met there the vision of Christ.

The afternoon sun was filling the courtyard of the Holy Sepulchre when I made a second visit to that puzzling collection of churches.

It is, at first difficult to understand its confusing topography. It is, in essentials, a round church, with the tomb of Christ in the centre of it. A large crusading choir leads from it, round which cluster a series of chapels. Some distance away, and fourteen feet higher than the rest of the church, is a chapel built over the holy hill of Golgotha. There is another church connected with, and behind, the choir, known as Saint Helena's Chapel, from which steps lead down into a rock cistern where the mother of Constantine discovered the Cross. But the two main sites on which the Church of the Holy Sepulchre have been built are the hill of Golgotha, or Calvary, and the garden tomb of St. Joseph of Arimathaea which was "in the place where he was crucified."

The church gives one an overwhelming impression of darkness and decay. There were passages so dark that I had to strike matches to find my way. And the decay everywhere of stone, of wood and of iron was fantastic. I saw pictures that were rotting on their canvases and I even saw canvases, still framed, that were bleached white: the last fragments of paint had peeled off, but they were still in position. There were ominous cracks and fissures in stone and marble. I thought how odd it is that extreme devotion can have exactly the same effect as extreme neglect. The Church of the Holy Sepulchre wears its air of shabby decay for the simple reason that the re-hanging of a picture, the repair of a stone, and even the mending of a window, assume such gigantic importance in the eyes of the communities that they provoke a situation capable of indefinite postponement.

What an incredible confusion of pillars and passages, of underground caves and semi-underground tunnels, has descended to us over sixteen centuries of battle and burning! It is an extraordinary muddle, and no one can understand this church in one or two visits. It is a labyrinth of passages and chapels embracing the three main shrines.

I ascended and descended steps and, led on by the light of glimmering tapers, explored dark galleries and pitch-black corridors. Once I was brought to a halt by kneeling Franciscans who were visiting the

Mother and child, girl and boy – the generations pass and change

Aqaba (above) shows a very different face from the street seller (right) in Jerusalem

candle-light on the over-burdened altars. Art and vulgarity stand side by side. A priceless chalice, the gift of an emperor, stands next to something tawdry and tinselly that might have been pulled from a Christmas tree. And hundreds of ikons, glimmering in old gold, receive candle drippings on the stiff Byzantine figures of saint and king.

The Greek monks swing their censers towards the blaze of candle-light and the blue clouds of their incense spurt out to hang about the ikons and the gilded screens. The worshippers, kneeling on the marble floors, seem to be prostrate before a series of exotic jewellers' shops. Only in the chapel of the Franciscans is there that chastity of decoration which one associates with a Western church. It is plain and rather chilly. It strikes at once the note that divides the Western from the Eastern Church in the Holy Land. Those who associate the Church of Rome with outward gorgeousness of vestment and ritual find in Jerusalem that the Latins are the staid and dowdy "Protestants," in brown robes girded with a rope, while the Greeks and the Armenians go garmented in scarlet and gold, with crosses of crystal and precious stones carried before them and incense in clouds about them.

Ascending a dim flight of steps, I found myself kneeling on a marble floor with a crowd of hushed people, each one of whom carried a lit candle. The person next to me sighed as though his, or her, heart

stations of the Cross, the light from their tapers shining on devout bearded faces which might have come from the walls of El Greco's house in Toledo. The first impression of the church is of a series of treasure caves. It is unlike the most ornate Roman Catholic church in Italy or Spain. Its richness and flamboyance are those of the Orient. It is as though the spoils of Asia Minor, of Russia and of Greece, accumulating for centuries, have been heaped in

103

were breaking. I stole a look and saw a black Nubian face, the white eyeballs shining in the candle-light, but whether the person was man or woman I could not tell because of the voluminous folds of drapery in which he, or she, was concealed.

We knelt before an altar that shivered in yellow candlelight and glittered with golden lamps and ikons. Divided from this chapel by two pillars, was a similar chapel before which the Franciscans were kneeling,

the candle-light moving over their devout, uncomplicated faces. We formed two congregations, kneeling together and facing the same way, but worshipping before separate chapels.

This was the hill of the Crucifixion: Calvary, the holiest place on earth. I looked round, hoping to be able to detect some sign of its former aspect, but that has been obliterated for ever beneath the suffocating trappings of piety. The chapel before which I was kneeling was the Chapel of the Raising of the Cross; the chapel next to it was the Chapel of the Nailing to the Cross.

When the crowd thinned, I approached nearer to the altar. There was a Greek priest there, watching the candles, snuffing some and lighting others. He beckoned me to come near the altar and pointed out a silver disc edged with candle grease and, below it, a hole in the rock in which, he whispered to me, the Cross of our Lord was fixed. The pilgrims came up, weeping and praying, to touch the rock with trembling fingers; and I went away wishing that we might have known this place only in our hearts.

The sun rises over Jerusalem from behind the Mount of Olives. I turned my back on the city and, looking up over the Mount, saw a great fan of light pulsing up from the east. The fire filled the sky and turned the little clouds in its path to pink and gold, but the

high ridge of the Mount, almost black against the palpitating light, hid the sun from view. Swifts flew screaming through the air. The noise they made as they darted over the Mount of Olives made me think of summer evenings at home in England. These birds, I believe, migrate to Europe from Africa and fill the air of the Holy Land with their high, bright screaming throughout the early months of the year. Hundreds of them cut the air like darts, swooping suddenly into the Valley of the Kedron and flying up again to dart and scream above the ochre-brown walls of Jerusalem.

The sun topped the crest of the Mount of Olives and, looking again towards Jerusalem, I saw the highest buildings gilded with light though the wall was yet unlit. In a few seconds a flood of light fell over the city, ran down the wall and into the Valley of the Kedron. It swept up the stony flanks of the opposite valley, and I felt my face and my hands warm in its light.

How often Jesus and the disciples must have watched this splendid sight from the Mount of Olives. They must have seen the city ramparts light up with the first rays of the sun. They must have seen, just above the Garden of Gethsemane, the towering white and gold mass of the Temple. They must have seen a priest come out on a pinnacle, as he came every morning, to look towards the east and report, before the first sacrifice of the day, "The sun shineth already!" They might even have heard in the still air of dawn the daily cry from the assembled priests: "Is the sky lit up as far as Hebron?", and the daily response of the watcher from the pinnacle: "It is lit up as far as Hebron!" Then, before the sun was warm among the olive trees, there would sound a shrilling of silver trumpets announcing that the first sacrifice of the day had been offered on the altar of burnt offerings. Up the slopes of the Mount of Olives would steal the smell of incense. . . .

תחנת הסעה
לחיילים

Utility in Jerusalem: the head as a vehicle (left) and a modern bus stop (above) in Hazanim Street

above: a time-honoured
form of transport in
Jerusalem

right: a Yemenite
soldier near the
Hazanim Street bus
stop

I went down into the valley, past the tomb of Absalom, and, climbing the narrow white track that runs up over the mounds and ruins of Zion, walked back beneath the walls. And from a minaret just above my head the muezzin came out, lifting his voice in the first call to prayer.

I joined the crowds one morning near the Jaffa Gate to watch the Hebron pilgrims march through Jerusalem during the Feast of Nebi Musa. This Moslem festival always coincides with the Holy Week of the Eastern Church. Devout pilgrims, accompanied by a number of fanatical dervishes, march through Jerusalem and, with sacred banners waving, go down to the Dead Sea to pay homage at a white-domed shrine which they believe to be the tomb of Moses. They camp out there for a week and then return to their villages. The history of this feast is curious.

The Moslems relate a legend that Moses, becoming lonely in his grave, complained to God, who promised him an annual pilgrimage. Another story is that, although Moses was one hundred and twenty years old, God told him that he should never die until he willingly stepped into the grave. Whereupon Moses began to tread softly in case he should step into a grave by mistake. One day, however, tired and hot, he came over the Mountains of Moab, where he saw four workmen who had made a deep cutting in

overleaf: The Dome of the Rock – "It is a dim, eight-sided building whose dome is erected on columns of magnificent porphyry, breccia and other tinted stones, all of them picked up by the Moslems from the ruins of Roman Jerusalem"

*Approach to the Dome
of the Rock*

*right: The Wailing
Wall – "an enormous
tawny stretch of wall
from whose cracks grow
tufts of grass and wild
caper plants"*

the rock. He asked what they were doing and they told him that they had made a hiding-place for a king's treasure. Moses, thinking that the cave looked cool and pleasant, entered and lay down on a ledge of rock. The workmen offered him a fruit of beautiful colour and of exquisite fragrance, but no sooner had he placed it to his lips than a deep sleep came over him. The four workmen, who were angels in disguise, then carried his soul into heaven.

The real history of the tomb of Moses is, I regret to say, not so picturesque. It appears that long ago the Turkish Government, alarmed by the enormous Christian crowds who flocked to the Holy Fire, determined to have an equal body of Moslems in the neighbourhood during the same period. Therefore the hitherto humble shrine of some obscure holy man near the Dead Sea was promoted into the tomb of Moses, and an annual pilgrimage organised to it.

The sun beat down on a crowd that pulsed and hummed with vitality. Hundreds of women, their faces hidden to the eyes in veils, lined the road and sat on walls, waiting. Peasants from all parts of the country wore vivid festival costumes. Lemonade sellers strolled through the crowd clapping their brass cups together and praising the coolness and the sweetness of the liquids. Men bearing trays of almond sweets, others with lettuces and some with coloured eggs, moved busily here and there; and from the distance came the throbbing of drums and beating of cymbals.

Slowly, and with but little organisation, the head of the procession came into sight. The leaders bore the sacred flags of silk, tasselled and embroidered and decorated with handkerchiefs tied to the poles, the votive-offering of village women. Each flag was carried by a member of a family whose cherished privilege it is to do so. Any attempt to interfere with this right would lead to instant bloodshed.

There was a flash of swords in the sunlight. The straggling procession halted. A ring was formed round two men armed with swords and bucklers. They executed a movement, half dance and half fight, hitting their bucklers by agreement, one-two, one-two, just like actors in a Shakespearean duel. The crowds applauded loudly.

Then came groups of wild haired fanatics who drugged their senses with a weird dance and a phrase known as the *Zikr*, or "the mentioning." It was a rhythmic repetition of the words "Lâ illálah ílla llâh . . . lâ illálah ílla llâh . . . lâ illálah ílla llâh . . ." — "there is no God but God." The effect of this repetition, and the shuffling dance that accompanied it, seemed to make them drunk. They sagged at the knees, wiped the sweat from their faces, tossed their wild hair, and all the time their lips moved in the "mentioning" and their eyes were vague and trance-like.

There were other bands intent on a different kind of excitement. They were mounted on the shoulders of their friends and were rushed rapidly up and down a clear space in the procession, beating time with their hands or with sticks like choir-masters, and

*Pause for thought, in old
Jerusalem*

from the Old Testament. This was the way the Hebrew fanatics danced and cried out against the Philistines and the Canaanites. The antics of dignified elderly Moslems, who came gyrating at the head of their villagers to the sound of timbrels and of hand-clapping, were surely those of David:

"And as the Ark of the Lord came into the city of David, Michal Saul's daughter looked through a window and saw King David leaping and dancing before the Lord; and she despised him in her heart."

It seemed to me that this procession of Nebi Musa preserved the atmosphere and the appearance of the crowds that came "singing unto Zion" for the great festivals of the year. It was a crowd like this, a crowd of excited, turbulent peasants, that congested the streets of Jerusalem when Christ joined the pilgrimage at Passover time. It was a mob like this that cried "Crucify Him!"

The Dome of the Rock, which is wrongly called the Mosque of Omar, is one of the most startling places I have ever seen. It is startling because, shining like a spectre through this great shrine of Islam, is a reflection of the Temple of Herod. I cannot understand how it is that the hundreds of books and guide-books about Jerusalem have neglected what I consider to be the most significant thing about this place. When you visit the Dome of the Rock you are visiting the ghost of the Temple in whose courtyards Jesus preached, and from whose gates He drove the hucksters.

This shrine is unquestionably the most exquisite building in Jerusalem and you will find ecstatic accounts of it in every book written about the city. It is a dim, eight-sided building whose dome is erected on columns of magnificent porphyry, breccia and other tinted stones, all of them picked up by the Moslems from the ruins of Roman Jerusalem. Most of the columns are still fitted with their Byzantine capitals, and a few of them are still marked with the sign of the cross.

I looked back from the depths of the Kedron Valley, but I could see only the tawny wall of Jerusalem towering above me on its rocky platform. As I began to climb the Mount of Olives, first a minaret, then a dome or two, appeared above the wall. Near the top of the Mount the whole city lay before me, slightly tilted in the direction of the Mount of Olives like an immense relief map that was slowly sliding into the abyss of the valley.

My first thought was amazement that Jerusalem should ever have been built. A more unlikely place for a famous city cannot be imagined. The arid mountains lie about it, rolling in long brown ridges against the sky, and in the valley below is only one spring of water—the Fountain of the Virgin. Jerusalem's water comes today, as it did in Old

chanting something to which the crowd responded with enthusiasm. I asked a man next to me what they were saying.

"They are cursing the Zionists," he replied. "They are singing: 'O Zionists what right have you in this country? What have you in common with us? If you stay in this country you will all find graves.'"

This gave me the clue to the whole procession. It was not an Arab procession at all! It was something

Testament times, from Solomon's Pools near Hebron. Water is also pumped from Ain Fara, the traditional "still waters" of the twenty-third Psalm. To-day, as in olden times, every drop of rain that falls on this high mountain ridge is saved in deep rock cisterns. There is a splendid defiance about the situation of Jerusalem, or perhaps it would be more correct to say that no people who did not believe themselves to be in the special care of God would have dared to have built a city in defiance of all the laws of prudence.

And my second thought was that never had I seen a more intolerant looking city. All the hardness of the rock and the smouldering fires within the rock seemed to have boiled up out of the bowels of the earth and cooled into the city of Jerusalem. It was a perfect expression, so it seemed to me, of the cruelty and the fierceness of the Judaean highlands. This high city, perched above ravines and lying among the débris of centuries, might, it seemed, be the abode not of men and women and children, but the dwelling-place of ruthless emotions such as Pride and Arrogance and Hate. And as I sat for a long while looking down on Jerusalem, I thought to myself: "That is undoubtedly the place that crucified Jesus Christ." Like an echo to my thought came a terrible reply: "And it would probably do so again."

The longer I looked at Jerusalem, the more I felt convinced that my first impression was not over-drawn or extravagant. If Jerusalem has not been born out of volcanic lava, she has at least been born from the fire of men's minds. Splendid and terrible things have happened behind her walls. The modern world was born in their shadow. Strange that the greatest event in the history of Mankind should have occurred on this bare plateau; stranger still, perhaps, that Jerusalem should still wear her historic air of intolerance. I seemed to hear a Voice in the pulse of the heat, and the Voice said:

"O Jerusalem, Jerusalem, thou that killest the prophets, and stonest them which are sent unto thee, how often would I have gathered thy children together, even as a hen gathereth her chickens under her wings, and ye would not!"

The words beat against my brain like an echo of the heat that quivered above the Mount of Olives. I listened again, but there was no sound but the thrusting of a plough through the dry soil and the click of a mule's hoof against a flint.

The Mount of Olives is slightly higher than Jerusalem, and stands up therefore like a screen between the city and the desert land that falls to the Dead Sea.

Jerusalem is 2,500 feet above sea level; the Dead Sea is 1,290 feet below sea level. So that in the course of about twenty-five miles the land falls nearly 4,000 feet into the hot, tropical world of the Jordan Valley. While it is frosty at night on the Jerusalem hills, it is hot and stuffy twenty-five miles away in Jericho, for the Jordan Valley is a phenomenal crack in the earth's surface which is filled with fierce heat

all the year round.

From the top of the Mount of Olives the view into this tropical trench looked like a photograph of the mountains of the moon. I gazed down into an apparently sterile world, a world of brown, domed hills piled together, bare of vegetation, and falling rapidly into the hot distance where a streak of blue marked the waters of the Dead Sea. Beyond the blueness rose a barrier of brown hills streaked with violet shadows.

"I look up and see the great yellow wall of Jerusalem and the walled-up Golden Gate, the site of the triumphal entry into the city"

117

They were the Mountains of Moab.

This was a view that Jesus knew well, and it has not altered since His eyes gazed upon it. He saw it when He came over the hill from Bethany or Bethphage and, no doubt, He turned, as every traveller turns, to look once more upon its superb indifference before, breasting the ridge, the view was hidden and Jerusalem came into sight.

How could Jerusalem fail to be the Holy City with this terrifying breeding-place of prophets before its eyes? The Golden Age of Israel was in the desert, when God took His people by the hand and led them safely into the Promised Land. It is this breath from the pure, sterilised desert that blows through the denunciation of Elijah and, in fact, through the denunciations by all those holy men who tried to lead Israel away from foreign cults and luxuries back to the old austerity. And I wondered, as I looked down on the silent, dead hills, whether Jesus loved to sleep in Bethany because, after the wrangling in the Temple court, He could catch a glimpse, as He crossed the Mount of Olives on His way back in the evening, of the calm "desert place" dedicated for ever to God.

I came down from the Mount of Olives. The noonday sun burned above Jerusalem. I saw the city lying compactly within its wall, modern Jerusalem scattered round it in clumps of white stone buildings. And the colour of old Jerusalem is the colour of a lion-skin. There are tawny yellows and dark browns and pale golds. It must have looked very like this when Jesus saw it in the time of Herod Antipas: a city like a lion crouched in the sun, watchful, vindictive, and ready to kill.

left: "They wore low, wide-brimmed black felt hats, and many of them were pale, spectacled and peering"

"Both Jews and Moslems believe that the Last Judgment will be held in the arid Valley of the Kedron, between Jerusalem and the Mount of Olives"

overleaf: "I saw the city lying compactly within its wall, modern Jerusalem scattered round it in clumps of white stone buildings.

And the colour of old Jerusalem is the colour of a lion-skin"

Images of Heaven and Hell

ALL TRAVELLERS IN the Holy Land repeat with monotonous regularity the true statement that the history of the country is "writ in water." Roads, villages, and even cities have disappeared from the map, but the spring that gushes out of the rock remains a constant factor in the life of the country and a true landmark to the historian.

In attempting to reconstruct the busy life of the Sea of Galilee as Jesus saw it, we must also remember that the hills, now so stark and bare, were at that time covered with trees. An intricate system of aqueducts, whose ruins are to be seen here and there (notably in some rocks at the back of the hospice at Tabgha), carried streams of fresh water wherever they were required. The climate must have been less fever-ridden than it is to-day. Possibly the wooded hills attracted a greater rainfall and also tempered the heat. One must think of this beautiful blue lake barred by a rampart of brown barren hills to the east, and ringed on the western shore with an almost unbroken chain of little towns lying at the foot of green hills thick with woods, bright with gardens, and loud with the music of running water.

I stood in the stillness of the morning looking down on the garden. The sun, rising from behind the Gergesene Hills, was climbing into the cloudless sky, and the garden was a network of sunlight and shade and full of the little early morning noises, the squeakings, the rustlings, the sound of wings, the cooing of pigeons and, from a fountain buried under trailing flowers, the falling of water.

The years fell shivering away from me and I was at that moment a small boy again, up and awake before anyone, looking out on the lovely world. I seemed to be a part of it and it seemed to be a part of me. The blue kingfisher, balancing himself on the very top of a fir tree, had come to say good-morning to me, and the little black lizard on the path who, seeing me move, had stopped dead in his tracks with his head lifted, he also, sharing this moment, shared fellowship. The same joy in life that used to send me running over the meadows at sun-rise, that would draw me to the corner of woods where the rabbits played, and to the edge of streams where the trout lay, drove me now to feel and to touch the morning, and to hold it in my arms. I flung a towel over my shoulder and went down the garden to a path cut through rocks at the edge of the lake. It ran south into a dark wood of eucalyptus trees that melted into the broad deserted Plain of Gennesaret.

There was not a soul to be seen. At the edge of the wood a stream of fresh water flowed from a pool overhung by precipitous crags. The pool was very still and deep. I flattened myself against a tree trunk and watched two kingfishers diving. They flew in circles over the pool and would suddenly begin to flutter in the air, at the same time pointing their long beaks towards the water until they looked like poised darts. Then they would drop like stones. They would touch the water swiftly and lightly and rise again; and, as they wheeled, the sun would shine a moment on the little silver fish in their beaks. The stones were covered with water tortoises. They looked like mud puddings, some dark from the water, others light and sun-dried. When I moved, they slid softly from their rocks into the pool.

The edge of the wood near the lake was a narrow half-moon of shingle. I stepped from my clothes and walked into the Sea of Galilee. The water was painfully cold, but I liked it. The stones underfoot were hard, but I did not mind them. I walked on and on into the shallow water. The sun was warm on my body but my knees were in ice. Soon it was deep enough to swim. I hugged myself in cowardice for a moment and then went in. The water was no longer cold and I struck out towards the Gergesene hills, which rose up from the lake with the morning shadows dark and clear on their sides. I swam back slowly. To the left I could see the shore curving south to Tiberias. I could see the little cluster of white boxes that was the town. In front of me was the green Plain of Gennesaret and the dark belt of the eucalyptus trees. The sensuous, satisfying touch of the water, the beautiful blue water, was ecstasy on this enchanted morning. I heard a clapping in the air and, lying on my back, watched the flock of white pigeons from Tabgha wheeling against the sky. And there was a little silver moon that I had not noticed until then, lying on its back against the blue.

I ran back to Tabgha. And there was honey for breakfast.

One morning I decided to "run down to Jericho," as they say in Jerusalem. They talk about Jericho as a Londoner might talk about Brighton. "Have you run down to Jericho yet?" is one of the first questions they ask the stranger, and at every dinner-party someone is sure to offer to "run you down" for a moonlight bathe in the Dead Sea.

That enigmatic emptiness to the east of the Mount of Olives, which drops into an unearthly wilderness where a strip of intensely blue water receives the shadow of mauve mountains, has powerfully influenced the mentality of Jerusalem. Like a lighthouse on a hill, she has always watched the Dead Sea country with respect and fear, for who could say what might not come up out of the wilderness, like a ship out of the ocean, to recall her to God?

To the Jewish theologian Jericho and the Jordan Valley were a portent, but to the modern geologist they are a freak. There is in all the world nothing quite like the contrast between the mountain city of Jerusalem, over 2,500 feet above the sea, and the Jordan Valley, only twenty-three miles away, sunk in a hot trench 1,300 feet below the sea. It is a climatic curiosity as fantastic as a strip of Brazilian jungle would be at the foot of Ben Nevis.

About three miles from Jerusalem a superb panorama of the Dead Sea country lay before me. I could see the white road twisting and turning into a sterile wilderness of parched rock, dropping ever

downward into bleakness and solitude. I stopped the car and got out.

I thought that I had never seen anything that looked more like the primitive conception of hell. It was the sort of place that an early Italian painter would have peopled with hairy little devils with horns and forked tails. The hillsides were either littered with millions of limestone chips or else they were bare and volcanic. Some of the hills were domed or cone-shaped like young volcanoes and others were queerly twisted, tortured and deformed as if chewed up by fire like the clinkers that come out of a furnace.

When I left the Inn of the Good Samaritan I plunged down into a land of fire. There was no shade anywhere. The sun beat in my eyes and quivered over the barren earth. In a little over half an hour I had left a temperate climate for the heat of the tropics.

Coming to a convenient place, I stopped the car and removed my coat, for I was suffocating. I looked into the abyss, where far below, cut in the side of a sand-coloured mountain, was a monastery built like a swallow's nest on the wall of a house. The cliffs round about this monastery were pitted with caves in which hermits still live, mortifying the flesh as they did in the Thebaid.

Onward I went down the blinding white road. There was a post with "Sea Level" printed on it; and the road still plunged downward, the heat growing even fiercer. A lizard streaked across the path leaving a twisted trail in the fine white dust. A movement on a hill revealed a group of camels, queer prehistoric-looking creatures the very colour of the sandy rocks, grazing with their calves upon the spiky bushes and the unwholesome-looking thorns. Turning a corner, I saw below me a view of the Jordan Valley and of Jericho among its trees and, to the right, the sparkling blue waters of the Dead Sea with the Mountains of Moab, streaked and slashed with shadows, rising from its eastern shores.

Some writers have described this hot gash in the earth's crust as the most horrible place in the world, while others have found it strangely beautiful. It is, I suppose, a matter of temperament or, perhaps, liver. If you are not feeling too well, I can imagine

that the Jordan Valley with its overwhelming heat and its airlessness, and Jericho with its flamboyant vegetation, its reptiles and its insects, could be a terrible nightmare. Here, strangely enough, is the same awful sterility which is encountered only on the summit of great mountains. Just as a man venturing alone above the vegetation belt on a high mountain is sometimes seized with a chill of terror, feeling that he is trespassing in the workshop of God, so in

*Cracked earth, pounded
into sterility by the
feet of sheep, and the
lushness of the Hula
nature reserve*

gloom is entirely false and reflects, perhaps, not the Dead Sea but the minds of those gallant voyagers. The story that no birds can fly across it because of poison in the air is also untrue. There are not many birds because there are no fish in the sea. The few Jordan fish that do get carried into the salt lake are soon cast up mummified on the shores. But the Dead Sea itself is as blue and as sparkling as Loch Lomond or Killarney on a summer's day.

The waters lap the beach of pebbles in oily little waves. There are no shells on the beach, no evidence of any life, no growth of weeds or water plants, for the waters are sterile and dead. The reason why the Dead Sea is a huge cauldron of chemicals is because there is no outlet. It is a vast hole in the earth into which the Jordan and tributary streams pour every day nearly seven million tons of water mixed with sulphurous and nitrous matter. Unable to escape, and subjected to the tremendous heat of the Jordan Valley, this water evaporates, leaving behind enormous deposits of salts and other chemicals in the sea. In the sea-bed there are also hot springs about which little is known. Ordinary sea-water holds from four to six per cent. of solids in solution; Dead Sea water holds five times as much. It is impossible for a bather to sink in it and a non-swimmer out of his depth cannot drown as long as he keeps his head. When Titus came to the Jordan Valley in 70 A.D. he caused several slaves to be chained together and flung into the Dead Sea. But they evidently kept their heads, for they emerged alive.

Any horror inspired by the Dead Sea is due to its appalling setting: the obscene banks of chemical

"It is as though this frightful judgment on human sin has for ever blasted and unhallowed the shores of the Dead Sea"

"The road to Hebron goes to the south out of Bethlehem into a wilderness of brown hills"

130

slime, the grey landslides of salt, the smell of sulphur, the weird, twisted foothills stained and tortured like the deposit at the bottom of a crucible. The hills are not shaped like ordinary hills: they are more like the fantastic outlines of cooled metal. As one wanders along the desolate shores the fate of Sodom and Gomorrah, which one may, possibly, have thought of as a tragic allegory, becomes terrifyingly real. It is as though this frightful judgment on human sin has for ever blasted and unhallowed the shores of the Dead Sea.

Pitchers for sale in
Hebron market

Passover, Crucifixion and Resurrection

JERUSALEM WAS FILLED with the people of all nations. One heard French, German, Italian, English, Arabic, Yiddish and Hebrew in the course of one short walk through the streets. Droves of superior tourists who had come to gaze curiously on the rites of the Eastern Church were queerly mixed with humble Eastern Christians who firmly believed that the Holy Fire was soon to descend from heaven upon the Tomb of Christ. Opulent Jews from far away had come to eat the Passover in the City of David and Solomon. The Moslems were talking of the great pilgrimage to the tomb of Moses near Jericho.

The little booths near the Holy Sepulchre overflowed with incense and became festooned with the richest of candles. Large piles of shrouds appeared outside them on chairs. They were of the thinnest, cheapest linen and bore, printed in black, rough pictures of the Passion. I saw a peasant woman from, I think, Bulgaria, buy a shroud. Although they were all the same, she went from shop to shop examining them and fingering the miserable texture. It must have been force of habit.

In the dimness of Calvary a forest of candles burned; and all day long silent crowds knelt before the Tomb of Christ.

In the dark streets of the old city the Jews watched the moon of Nisan grow full, and went about their intricate preparations with an air of furtive secrecy. For the Passover was near.

Dean Stanley once said that travel in the Holy Land is like travel in the dark. You traverse great tracts of country with nothing to indicate any link with the past except that you tread the same ground and breathe the same air. Then suddenly a flash of lightning comes and for an instant tower, tree and field are seen as distinctly as in the broad daylight.

Jerusalem in the throes of its religious and political enthusiasms is such a flash. In the strange agglomeration of ignorance, cynicism, simple piety, sophistication, scholarship and stupidity which fills Jerusalem at this time, I seem to see a clear reflection of the Jerusalem of Christ.

If I could paint, I think that as I sit under the olives, looking at Jerusalem, I could put down on canvas the very city that Jesus saw when He came up to the Passover to be crucified. It was filled with the same varied crowds: uncouth provincials, simple Galileans, curious interested Greeks, prosperous Jews from Alexandria, sight-seeing Romans, white-robed priests and Levites, smooth Sadducees, obvious Pharisees with broad fringes to their garments and large phylacteries on their brows, and Roman soldiers in their helmets and their chestnut-coloured tunics, spear in hand.

It is not difficult to imagine the sights and sounds that surrounded Jesus as He came up for the great birthday feast of the Jews, the feast that commemorated the Exodus and drew all who could travel towards the Paschal communion at Jerusalem.

Its heralds were abroad in the land weeks before-hand. All the roads and bridges were repaired after the winter rains. Every sepulchre received its annual coat of whitening so that it shone in the sun, and thus lessened the risk of ceremonial defilement. Jesus, when He rebuked the scribes and Pharisees from the Temple mount, pointed to the rows upon rows of newly whitened sepulchres below Him on the slopes of the Mount of Olives and drew, as He so often did, a striking comparison with something visible going on around Him: "Ye are like unto whited sepulchres," He cried, drawing their attention to the shining tombs in their Passover whitewash, "which indeed appear beautiful outward, but are within full of dead men's bones, and of all uncleanliness." The sight of these whitened sepulchres was one of the characteristic signs that Passover was on the way.

The lanes of Jerusalem are striped like a tiger. You pass perpetually from strips of sunlight into bands of shadow. Some of the bazaars are vaulted. They exist in a stealthy twilight, the sun spirting down through cracks and holes in the roof as water spirts from a punctured water-skin. But most of them are open to the sky, the shadow of minaret, dome and tower flinging darkness over the cobbles and the walls.

One could write a book about walls. There are walls in Andalusia, in the south of Spain, which seem built as a barrier against lovers. There are walls in Tuscany which have been erected to keep out the assassin: and there are walls in England, like the walls of Hampton Court Palace, which seem made to hide from common eyes the pleasures of the privileged. But the walls in the old city of Jerusalem are unlike any walls I know. They have a furtiveness born of fear and uncertainty. They are high and mildewed and sunk in age. The doors in them seem built for dwarfs, and if you ring a bell, or bang one of the rusty iron hammers, it is almost certain that a grid will shoot open and an aged eye will look out at you before the bolt is shot.

Centuries of suspicion and persecution, during which Christians, their armies disbanded and scattered, held their own by the feminine qualities of guile and diplomacy, have cast a virginal terror over the walls of Jerusalem, almost as though every ringer of the bell, or every knocker at the gate, might be a ravisher of altars. All the beauty is carefully hidden behind these walls. They seem, in fact, deliberately ugly, as if to deceive the plunderer and, looking at them, one thinks of those holy nuns who mutilated their faces and cut off their noses in order to preserve their virtue when the barbarians thundered down on the last of the Roman Empire.

Sometimes, when a postern gate is open, you see beyond the stained wall to a cool paved courtyard lined with the stumps and pediments of old Roman columns. In the centre of the courtyard there may be a lemon tree, and beneath it an old monk reading a book. Then the door closes; and you wonder whether the brief glimpse of the peace on the other side was

true, or merely the vision of a sun-stricken brain.

As one plods over these narrow lanes in Jerusalem, the confusion of centuries presses on the mind. There is an overpowering solemnity in the memory of all the Jerusalems that lie underfoot. The Jerusalem of the Gospels was itself rooted in old bones. And the Jerusalems that have grown up and have vanished since the time of Christ—the Roman city of Hadrian, the early Christian city of Constantine, the Jerusalem of Omar, the Jerusalem of the Crusades, the Jerusalem of Saladin, the Jerusalem of Sulieman and the many Turkish Jerusalems—these, lying one upon another and thrusting their relics through the soil, almost strike terror into the mind. To walk through Jerusalem is to walk through history. Beneath one's feet and scattered around in every direction lie the bones of the Past.

As I went on through the old city, I was conscious also of a feeling of imprisonment. All the dark little lanes, the high, blank walls, and the jumbled buildings erected to the glory of God, are bound tightly together by a high city wall. The wall of Jerusalem, her armour and shield in time of trouble, still exerts a powerful influence on the mind and you are subconsciously aware of it every minute of the day. You are either inside the wall, acutely aware of its encircling embrace, or you are outside it, looking back at it, thinking that it clasps the city in its brown stone arms as if trying to shield it from the modern world.

I came by way of narrow street and blank wall, by sunlight and by shadow, to the ancient Gate of St. Stephen. I saw, framed in the graceful Saracenic arch of its stones, a brilliant little picture of the world

The Via Dolorosa

"I came into a Jerusalem that in my absence had changed. Its streets were full of pilgrims from East and West, for in a few days it would be Easter, the Passover, and the Feast of Nebi Musa"

beyond the wall. I sighed with relief at the sight of so much air and openness, so much sky, and mountains with the sun over them. And the hill-side that rose up opposite was the Mount of Olives.

All my life I have had a picture of the Mount of Olives in my mind, a picture composed by my own imagination and influenced by illustrations in books and by canvases in art galleries; but it was a very different picture from the reality. I had always thought of the Mount of Olives as an improbable hill, with plenty of tall cypress trees among belts of woodland and little gardens with wells and fountains in them. But the real Mount of Olives is a bare ridge sloping up from the stricken-looking Kedron Valley; a ridge of rock on which the sun beats down all day long. There are white tracks twisting here and there among the rocks, and a few ploughed fields terraced in the rock and upheld on the hill by breast-high walls of limestone. In these fields are a few stumpy olive trees.

In any other place the Mount of Olives would seem bare and inhospitable, but, in contrast to Jerusalem and the mountains by which it is surrounded, it is peaceful and gracious; the only place in which to-day, as in the time of our Lord, you could go to sit under a tree and forget the nervous tension of the city.

Low down, just where the Jericho Road sends a branch road right up over the crest of the Mount of Olives, is a small patch of trees within a wall. I

138

"Jerusalem was filled with the people of all nations. One heard French, German, Italian, English, Arabic, Yiddish and Hebrew in the course of one short walk through the streets"

that every tree on the Mount of Olives was hewn down to make crosses and assault-ladders. Later, when the Jews opposed Hadrian, the Emperor authorised five hundred crucifixions a day.

There were three kinds of crosses: the *crux decussata* shaped like an X, also called the *crux Andreana*, because it was on this form of cross that St. Andrew was crucified at Patrae; the *crux commissa*, or St. Anthony's Cross, which was shaped like the letter T; and the *crux immissa* of Christian tradition, which had a head-piece projecting above the cross-bar.

Half-way up the upright wood of the cross was a slight projection known as the *sedile*, or seat, or as the *cornu*, or horn. This took part of the victim's weight, which would otherwise have been too great to have depended entirely on the outstretched hands. It is not known whether there was a foot-rest. Sometimes, it appears, the victim's feet were nailed to the cross, at others it seems they were merely bound with cords. Death was always a lingering doom. The victim was left to sob the days away, exposed to the sun, torn by pain, hunger, and thirst, until his executioners, becoming weary of his agony, despatched him with the *crurifragium*, or the breaking of the legs.

Crucifixions were always executed outside city gates and in prominent places near high roads in order that publicity might be given to the agony of the condemned and to the crime for which he had

"It is an extraordinary
muddle, and no one can
understand this church
in one or two visits. It is
a labyrinth of passages
and chapels embracing
the three main shrines"

*following pages: Old
and modern Jerusalem*

been sentenced. It was quite usual to leave the main upright of the cross in position on a recognised place of execution and the only other portion necessary, the cross-beam, was carried by the victim on his shoulders to the place of death. Artists are wrong in picturing our Lord bowed beneath the weight of the entire cross.

Most modern artists err also in giving too great a height to the cross. It was considered sufficient if the victim's feet just cleared the ground. If the cross on which our Lord suffered had been as high as most artists imagine, it would not have been possible for the soldier to have offered the sponge of vinegar on a short reed.

In Jerusalem a society of charitable women provided a merciful drug for those about to be crucified. It was administered just before the victim, stretched on the ground, was nailed to the cross-beam. The inspiration for this act of compassion was the ordinance in *Proverbs*, chapter thirty-one, verse six:

"Give strong drink unto him that is ready to perish."

It is believed that the potion offered by these women was a mixture of wine and drugs, including frankincense, laudanum, myrrh, resin, saffron and mastich. This is "the wine mingled with myrrh" mentioned by St. Mark. It was offered to Jesus before the Crucifixion, but "he received it not."

In Judaea the usual practice of crucifixion was modified in deference to the Jewish law, which forbade a victim to hang on the cross all night. The bodies had, therefore, to be taken down before evening in order that the ground might not suffer pollution, because everyone who suffered death on "the tree" was, according to *Deuteronomy*, accursed. This explains the haste in which Jesus was condemned and executed, the early trial before Pilate, and the breaking of the thieves' legs in the early afternoon. Additional urgency was felt on this occasion because at six p.m. on the evening of the Crucifixion the Sabbath of Paschal week began.

The most shameful symbol of the ancient world has become the sacred emblem of the Christian Faith. In the days of the early Church the first Christians defended the cross from the sneers of the pagan by pointing out its universal presence in Nature and in everyday life: the wings of a flying bird, the branches of trees, the projecting oars of galleys, the ship's mast and yard, the yoke of a plough, the handle of a spade, the nose and eyebrows of the human face, and so on.

"If any man will come after me, let him deny himself and take up his cross and follow me."

With these words the cross took on a new and glorious meaning. The symbol of Death became the symbol of Life.

The *Via Dolorosa* was mercifully short—scarcely a thousand paces. It lay from the Praetorium to the Gate Genath. Outside this gate, and a few yards from the city wall beside the main road into Jerusalem

from the north, stood a place called Golgotha, the Place of a Skull. There is nothing in any of the four Gospels to suggest that Golgotha was a hill, but it has been assumed that it must have been so. The first person to call it a hill was the Bordeaux Pilgrim, who visited Jerusalem in 333 A.D., when the Church of the Holy Sepulchre was being built. He mentioned "the little hill of Golgotha (*monticulus Golgotha*) where the Lord was crucified."

For hundreds of years after Latin writers continued to refer to Golgotha as "the rock of the cross" or "the rock of Golgotha," and it was not until the sixth century that again the idea of elevation was associated with it, and we read of "Mount Calvary." By this time, of course, the original elevation had long been disguised by architects.

Those who thronged the streets near the Praetorium would have seen the terrible, but familiar, procession of death. A centurion in charge of a half maniple of the Twelfth Legion came first, riding on horseback and clearing a path through the narrow streets. Behind him walked a legionary bearing a notice board on a pole. Written in red on a background of white gypsum was a brief account of the crimes committed by those about to die.

Jesus followed, bearing His cross-beam, clothed no longer in the scarlet gown of the mockery but, as St. Matthew tells us, in His own raiment. There is an old tradition that He wore a black robe girded at the waist with a leather belt and that under it was the rich vestment given to Him in derision by Herod. He did not wear the crown of thorns, which was carried by one of the executioners in order that He might be crowned again on the cross. Worn out with suffering and with emotion, our Lord was unable to keep pace with the procession, and it seems that in the pressing into service of Simon, the Cyrenian, we may detect a touch of kindness on the part of the centurion, Longinus, who was soon to testify to the Divinity of his Prisoner and to embrace the Christian faith.

The two thieves followed, bearing the cross-beams; and behind them, marching six to the rank, came the remainder of the half maniple, spear on shoulder. The Sanhedrists, who wished no doubt to enjoy their triumph, followed at the end of the procession, but, when they came to the Gate Genath, kicked their white mules into a canter and went on ahead to Golgotha.

In the sunlight of a spring morning, when the swifts were flying above the walls of Jerusalem as they do to this day in the month of Nisan, three crosses were set up outside the city gate. Those who were "looking on afar off" covered their eyes and stood with breaking hearts. And the hours wore on. The soldiers beneath the Cross shook dice in a helmet for the seamless coat. They lay down on Golgotha in the heat of the day to eat bread and cheese and to drink their sour wine. They heard the Divine words of compassion break from the lips of the Lonely Man:

"Father, forgive them; for they know not what they do."

At three o'clock in the afternoon the Sanhedrists went to Pilate to demand the *crurifragium* in order that the bodies might not hang on the cross until the evening, which also was—how little they knew it—the beginning of a new day. And the soldiers hastened the death of the two thieves, "but when they came to Jesus, and saw that he was dead already, they brake not his legs."

The Tomb of Jesus Christ is a small cell lined with marble, six and a half feet long, and six feet wide. Only two or, at the most, three people can enter at one time. On the right hand is a cracked slab of white marble, three feet in height, covering the rock on which He was placed after the Crucifixion.

From the marble roof of this tiny cell hang lamps which belong in various proportions to the Greek, Latin, Armenian and Coptic Churches. The Roman Catholics are known in Palestine as the Latins. Standing at the head of the marble slab was an impassive Greek monk with a soft, spade-shaped black beard. He wore a black cassock and a high, black, rimless hat, beneath which his hair was pinned at the back in a round bun. He held a bunch of candles in his hand and, as the pilgrims entered, gave one to them, which they lit from others burning in the tomb.

I could see a pilgrim kneeling at the sepulchre, so I waited in the small, dark ante-chamber outside.

Becoming impatient, I bent down and, peeping through the low entrance, saw that the man inside was an old, bent peasant in ragged clothes, his feet in a pair of huge shoes made of felt. He was a Bulgarian who had come over in a pilgrim ship, as the Russians used to come, and he had probably been saving up all his life for that moment.

He was kneeling at the marble slab and kissing it repeatedly, while tears ran down the deep wrinkles of his face and fell on the stone. His large, rough hands, the nails split and black with labour, touched the marble gently with a smoothing motion; then he would clasp them in prayer and cross himself.

He prayed aloud in a trembling voice, but I could not understand what he was saying. Then, taking from his pocket various pieces of dirty paper and a length of ribbon, he rubbed them gently on the Tomb and put them back in his pocket.

I thought there might perhaps be room for me, so I bent my head and entered the Sepulchre. The Greek monk, the kneeling peasant and myself quite filled the small space. And it would have been all right if the old man had continued to kneel, but, disturbed perhaps by my entrance, he rose up, the tears still falling, and whispered something to me. We were now standing, our chests touching, and, looking into his eyes, I realised that I was looking at real happiness.

This was his life's dream. I had never seen such happiness before. Never in all my life have I beheld

overleaf: a guard patrols the site of an archaeological dig on Mount Nebo

peace and contentment written so clearly on a human face. I would have given the world to have been able to speak to him, but we stood there in the Tomb of Christ, he whispering something to me which I did not understand, and I shaking my head.

He then turned from me towards the Greek monk and said the same thing to him. But the monk could not understand, and he also shook his head. The old man became frantic with anxiety. He raised his voice slightly and then, casting a swift glance towards the marble slab, lowered it, and pointed to his forehead and to the lamps that hang over Christ's Tomb. Then the monk understood. Nodding gravely, he lowered one of the lamps on a chain and taking a piece of cotton wool, he dipped it lightly in the oil of the lamp, and with this made the sign of the Cross upon the peasant's face.

The old man sank down on his knees and turned again to the Tomb, unwilling to leave, incoherent with faith and devotion, his big, scarred hands touching the marble lovingly as if stroking the hair of a child. Presently he backed out of the candle-light into the dim Chapel of the Angel.

The night before I left Jerusalem I went out into the streets of the old city. It was a lovely night and the moon was rising. Behind the Damascus Gate a flight of steps goes up to the city wall. Mounting the ramparts, I walked in the direction of Herod's Gate along the narrow path made for the bowmen of the Middle Ages.

The moon rose, steeping the city in a fall of green light. A breathless silence lay over Jerusalem. Each dome, tower and minaret was clearly etched against the sky; each tree stood in its own small pool of moonlight. Sometimes the sentry walk descended by steps to a lower level and mounted again; sometimes I entered guard houses set at intervals on the wall, small stone chambers through whose bow-slits I saw a narrow vision of the moonlit roads beyond the city. Crossing Herod's Gate, I came at length to the corner tower and, turning to the south, walked along the east wall that overlooks the Mount of Olives.

The moon hung above the Mount, touching the ridge with a gold haze, washing every white track in light, painting each olive tree in shadow against the rocks. How hushed it was in the light of the moon. Not a footstep rang in the streets below me; no one moved in the silence beyond the wall. Above the black shadow of the Kedron Valley I could see the moonlight silvering the trees in the Garden of Gethsemane. . . .

Upon the third day, early in the morning, Mary Magdalene hastened to the Tomb, and when she saw that it was empty sorrow filled her heart, so that, St. John tells us, she wept. As she turned to go, Some-one stood before her, and she heard a Voice asking:

"Woman, why weepest thou? whom seekest thou?"

"Sir, if thou have borne him hence," she begged, "tell me where thou hast laid him, and I will take him away."

"Mary."

"Master!"

Jesus instantly exhibited the strange difference that is noticeable in all his subsequent contact with the Apostles:

"Touch me not," He said gently, "for I am not yet ascended to my Father."

One imagines that Mary in her joy had flung her-self at the feet of Christ and had tried to touch Him.

"Go to my brethren." He commanded, "and say unto them I ascend unto my Father, and your Father; and to my God and your God."

In the greyness of the morning the woman ran back with the message that Christ had Risen.

"But when the morning was now come, Jesus stood on the shore: but the disciples knew not that it was Jesus"
(John 21:4)

Glossary

of place names mentioned by H. V. Morton

(Alternative names, ancient or modern, are included in parentheses)

Antioch (Antakya) – town in south-west Turkey. The disciples were first given the name 'Christians' here in AD42.

Bashan – a territory to the east of the Jordan and north of Gilead
Bethany (Bethana) – village high on the Mount of Olives, 2 miles outside Jerusalem
Bethany beyond Jordan – site not known
Bethlehem (Beit Lahm) – town in Jordan, scene of David's boyhood, and the birthplace of Jesus
Bethphage – village situated between Bethany and the summit of the Mount of Olives
Bethsaida Julias (El-Tell) – village lying on the banks of the Jordan where it flows into the Sea of Galilee. Jesus fed the 5,000 nearby

Caesarea – formerly great seaport of the Mediterranean, 28 miles north of Tel Aviv. It was built by Herod the Great.
Caesarea Philippi (Banias) – village in Syria at the foot of Mount Hermon
Capernaum – ancient city, usually identified with Tell Ham, on the north west shore of the Sea of Galilee. Its fine synagogue has been excavated and restored
Carmel, Mount – range of mountains running 18 miles south east from Haifa. The summit is said to be the spot where Elijah defeated the prophets of Baal.

Damascus (Esh-sham or Demashq) – modern capital of Syria. Scene of St Paul's conversion and of Mahomet's rejection of worldly pleasures
Dead Sea (Salt Sea, Bahr Lut (Arabic) = Sea of Lot) – lowest place on earth, lying between Israel and Jordan, 1292 feet below sea level. The Jordan empties itself into it. Sodom and Gomorrah, according to legend, lie beneath its waters.
Decapolis – the cities of Damascus, Dion, Gadara, Gerasa, Hippos, Kanatha, Pella, Philadelphia, Raphana and Scythopolis, which formed a league about 63BC as a defence against the Bedouin. Greek-speaking, they were subject to the Roman governor of Syria

Esdraelon, Plain of (Plain of Jezreel, Emek Jezreel) – separates the mountains of Samaria from those of Galilee, and is bounded on the west by Mount Carmel
Euphrates – longest river of the area, flowing about 1,700 miles from Turkey, through Syria and Iraq to the Gulf, after uniting with the Tigris

Galilee – region to the north of Samaria and west of the Sea of Galilee and a tetrarchy under the Herods
Galilee, Sea of (Lake of Gennesaret, Lake Tiberias) – lake through which the Jordan flows and upon whose shores Jesus preached
Gerasa – see Jerash
Gergesa (Kersa) – on eastern shores of the Sea of Galilee. It was down the nearby mountains that the Gadarene swine are believed to have stampeded.
Gennesaret, Plain of – lies on the western shores of the Sea of Galilee
Gilead – mountainous region to the east of the Sea of Galilee
Gomorrah – see Dead Sea
Good Samaritan, Inn of the (Khan Hathrur) – ancient building on the Jerusalem to Jericho road and quite probably the site of the inn mentioned in the biblical parable

Hermon, Mount (Jebel-esh-Sheikh) – mountain ridge on Lebanon, Syria, Israel border, above the sources of the Jordan

Jerash (Gerasa) – 20 miles east of the Jordan in the mountains of Gilead. Rebuilt by the Romans 63BC, possibly the site of Ramoth-gilead.
Jericho (Ariha) – in the Jordan valley, 15 miles from Jerusalem, and formerly an important city. Archaeological investigations tend to corroborate the biblical account of its destruction in the Late Bronze Age by Joshua.
Jezreel, Plain of – see Esdraelon, Plain of
Jerusalem – the ancient capital of the Holy Land, sacred to Jews, Christians and Muslims. Capital of the State of Israel. It is situated in wild hills, 2,500 feet above sea level.
Jordan – principal river of the Holy Land, following a winding course from the foot of Mount Hermon to the Dead Sea, a distance of about 160 miles, during which it falls some 3,000 feet.
Judaea – region south of Samaria and west of the Dead Sea

Moab, Hills of – plateau to the east of the Dead Sea

Nablus (Shechem) – town in Jordan, where Abraham set up camp upon entering Canaan, and to which Joshua brought the Israelites after crossing the Jordan. It is the main centre of the Samaritans.
Nazareth (al-Nasira) – town in Galilee where Jesus spent His boyhood, situated halfway between the Sea of Galilee and the Mediterranean
Nebo, Mount – the traditional site of Moses' death, to the east of the Dead Sea

Samaria (Sebastiye) – Ancient city, rebuilt by Herod the Great, and capital of the province, which is situated between Galilee and Judaea
Shechem – see Nablus
Sidon (Saida) – premier city of the Phoenicians, situated on the Mediterranean, south of Beirut
Sodom – see Dead Sea

Tiberias – town on west shore of the Sea of Galilee, the capital of Galilee, founded in AD26 by Herod Antipas
Tyre (Sur) – ancient town of Syria, formerly an important Phoenician port, now in Lebanon

Index